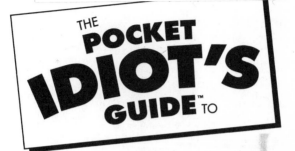

THE POCKET IDIOT'S GUIDE TO

Medicare Part D

by Lita Epstein, MBA

ALPHA

A member of Penguin Group (USA) Inc.

ALPHA BOOKS

Published by the Penguin Group

Penguin Group (USA) Inc., 375 Hudson Street, New York, New York 10014, USA

Penguin Group (Canada), 90 Eglinton Avenue East, Suite 700, Toronto, Ontario M4P 2Y3, Canada (a division of Pearson Penguin Canada Inc.)

Penguin Books Ltd., 80 Strand, London WC2R 0RL, England

Penguin Ireland, 25 St. Stephen's Green, Dublin 2, Ireland (a division of Penguin Books Ltd.)

Penguin Group (Australia), 250 Camberwell Road, Camberwell, Victoria 3124, Australia (a division of Pearson Australia Group Pty. Ltd.)

Penguin Books India Pvt. Ltd., 11 Community Centre, Panchsheel Park, New Delhi—110 017, India

Penguin Group (NZ), 67 Apollo Drive, Rosedale, North Shore, Auckland 1311, New Zealand (a division of Pearson New Zealand Ltd.)

Penguin Books (South Africa) (Pty.) Ltd., 24 Sturdee Avenue, Rosebank, Johannesburg 2196, South Africa

Penguin Books Ltd., Registered Offices: 80 Strand, London WC2R 0RL, England

International Standard Book Number: 978-1-59257-899-3
Library of Congress Catalog Card Number: 2009920702

11   10   09   8   7   6   5   4   3   2   1

Interpretation of the printing code: The rightmost number of the first series of numbers is the year of the book's printing; the rightmost number of the second series of numbers is the number of the book's printing. For example, a printing code of 09-1 shows that the first printing occurred in 2009.

Printed in the United States of America

Note: This publication contains the opinions and ideas of its author. It is intended to provide helpful and informative material on the subject matter covered. It is sold with the understanding that the author and publisher are not engaged in rendering professional services in the book. If the reader requires personal assistance or advice, a competent professional should be consulted.

The author and publisher specifically disclaim any responsibility for any liability, loss, or risk, personal or otherwise, which is incurred as a consequence, directly or indirectly, of the use and application of any of the contents of this book.

To my father, who helped me to learn all the details about using Medicare and how it works.

Contents

Appendix

Introduction

Medicare Part D partially solved a major problem—helping seniors pay for their drugs—but it also created a huge headache when it comes to picking out the right plan. While it's great that seniors have financial help to pay for the medications they need, the private insurance plan options are complex and hard to understand.

At the time of this writing, Congress was considering fixing the plan for 2010 to allow the government to negotiate lower drug prices for seniors and find a way to close the donut hole when seniors have no coverage for the drugs they need.

Whether or not Congress acts, this book will help you to understand the basics of the program—who's eligible, how the insurance companies can control your drug use, the costs involved, how you can enroll, and how you can make changes in the plan you chose. We also explore the marketing tactics private plans use—what they are allowed to do and what they can't.

Even if you are eligible for Medicare Part D, that doesn't mean you should sign up. You may have better coverage from somewhere else, like your retirement health plan from a former company or union, the Veteran's Administration, or your state's health benefits. So if you do get drug coverage from somewhere else, tread carefully before signing up for Medicare Part D. I explore who shouldn't apply in Chapter 2.

Finally, you'll find in Chapter 9 a screen-by-screen guide showing you how to use the Medicare.gov tool to help you choose the best plan for you based on the drugs you take. Hopefully all this information helps you to improve your ability to make use of the Medicare Part D benefit.

Extras

I've developed a few helpers you'll find in little boxes throughout the book:

def•i•ni•tion

These help you learn the language of Medicare Part D.

Drug Warnings

These give you warnings about things you need to avoid.

Drug Tips

These give you ideas for how to work with Medicare Part D and how to find the resources you need.

Acknowledgments

A special thanks goes to Randy Ladenheim-Gil, my executive editor at Alpha Books, for her continuing support of my work at the Penguin Group. Thanks also to Jennifer Bowles, my development editor, and Kayla Dugger, production editor, for their work in the editing and production of the book. In addition, I want to thank my agent Jessica Faust for her efforts to keep me working and, of course, I must thank my husband, H. G. Wolpin, for his support and encouragement for all that I do.

Trademarks

All terms mentioned in this book that are known to be or are suspected of being trademarks or service marks have been appropriately capitalized. Alpha Books and Penguin Group (USA) Inc. cannot attest to the accuracy of this information. Use of a term in this book should not be regarded as affecting the validity of any trademark or service mark.

What's Covered

In This Chapter

- Getting down to basics
- Coverage options
- Types of plans
- Premium prices
- Looking at the state roadmap

Your first question when you ask about the drug prescription benefit for Medicare is probably, "What's covered?" I wish this were an easy question to answer, but I can only say it depends upon the private insurance carrier you choose.

In 2006, Congress passed a law that specifies the basics for Medicare Prescription Drug Benefits, also called Part D, but the variables could make your head spin. In this chapter, we'll review the basics of that Congressional mandate and introduce you to some of the variables you'll need to consider as you start to choose the plan that is right for you.

Basics of Coverage

Every insurer must guarantee certain coverage as mandated by the government. Some plans offer more coverage if you want to pay for it. The greatest variability is in the list of drugs that are covered by each private insurer and the level of coverage for each of those drugs. In Chapter 2, we'll take a closer look at who qualifies for this drug coverage. We'll talk about people who may qualify but are better off staying with their current drug coverage and not signing up for Part D.

Before I get into the complexities of the options, let's take a look at the basic provisions in the law. Each senior 65 or older can voluntarily decide to enroll in a Medicare prescription drug plan. If a senior does enroll, she will pay a monthly premium for the plan to the private insurer chosen. In most cases, this premium will be taken out of the senior's Social Security check, but the premium can be paid for in other ways, which I discuss in Chapter 6.

A senior paid a deductible of $295 in 2009, which means seniors had to spend $295 on drugs before drug costs were covered. Some plans do have an option that offers coverage for this deductible. The deductible has gone up each year since passage of the law in 2006. In 2006, the deductible was $45 less—$250.

Once the deductible is met, the senior pays 25 percent of prescription costs and the insurer pays 75 percent of the costs. The 25 percent is the senior's *co-pay.* In 2009, seniors had coverage until they spent $601.25 out-of-pocket on drugs and receive $2,700 worth of drugs. These levels change each year. In 2006, when the program started, seniors had coverage until they spent $500 out-of-pocket and the total cost of their drugs was $2,250.

def•i•ni•tion

Co-pay is the amount of money a senior pays out-of-pocket for prescription drugs when she picks up the prescription.

After these benchmarks are met, seniors then lose all coverage until they spend another $3,453.76 out-of-pocket on drugs in 2009. This is what people call the donut hole, because seniors get $0 for the costs of their drugs at this point of coverage. A few plans do offer some coverage of generics for an extra premium. The maximum paid by each senior out-of-pocket was $2,850 when the coverage started in 2006.

Once a senior spends $4,350 out-of-pocket (that includes the $295 deductible, plus $601.25 co-pay, plus $3,453.75 in the donut hole) and the total value of drugs received is $6,153.75 ($295 deductible, plus $2,700 paid by insurer, plus $3,453.76 paid by senior once the donut hole was reached), then the senior will get catastrophic coverage and only pay 5 percent of all future drug costs and the insurer will pay 95 percent. The amount to be paid out-of-pocket will be adjusted yearly. This catastrophic coverage started after a total of $5,100 in drugs was received when the program started in 2006.

If the senior spent a total of $4,350 on drugs in 2009, he made it to the catastrophic coverage window. At that point, the senior spent $2.40 for a 30-day supply of *generic* or *preferred drugs* and $6 for a 30-day supply of all other drugs.

def•i•ni•tion

A **generic drug** is non-brand-name drug that is identical in dose, strength, route of administration, safety, efficacy, and intended use as the brand-name drug it copies.

A **preferred drug** is a drug that an insurer prefers be used for treatment and therefore, the insurer will pay a larger share of that drug's costs. This can include both generic and brand-name drugs.

Taking a Look at Options

If this isn't confusing enough, there are lots more options from which you can choose. That's because Congress decided to make this plan available through private insurers rather than directly from Medicare. Insurers were given great flexibility in how they could design their plans, provided they meet the minimum requirements discussed earlier in the chapter. Options from which you can choose include drugs that are covered, deductibles, co-pays, pharmacy of choice, and coverage in the gap or donut hole.

Specific Drugs Covered

As you search for plans, you will find great variability in the drugs that are covered. Each insurer decides upon its formulary, which is a list of drugs that are covered. In Chapter 4, I'll take a closer look at how drug formularies work and how the insurance companies are controlling the choice of drugs you can use.

Drug Warnings

The use of formularies by insurance companies is a common practice in health care today. If your doctor wants to prescribe a drug that is not on your insurer's formulary, you will have to pay more for that drug. In some cases, an insurance company will pay for part of the cost of a nonpreferred drug, but in other cases the insurer will decide not to cover the drug at all.

Deductible Options

Another common option is how much your deductible will be. The official rules, as set by Congress, were to have a deductible of $250 that would be adjusted for inflation. That deductible is already up to $295 and has gone up each year since the program started in 2006. Many private insurers do offer $0 deductible plans. In fact, of the 1,875 plans offered in 2009, 1,127 offered a $0 deductible option.

Drug Tips

Don't just look for $0 deductible plans. Be sure you look at the costs for each of the drugs you are taking before choosing a plan. Although a plan may offer a $0 deductible to attract customers, when you review the individual costs of your drugs you might find them higher on a $0 deductible plan.

Insurers know seniors don't like to pay a deductible, but be careful. You could actually end up paying more annually on a $0 deductible plan if that insurer doesn't cover your drugs or if your co-pays are higher. Chapter 5 takes a closer look at the costs of your plan choices.

Co-Pays

Your co-pays can have a significant impact on your total costs for prescription drugs in a year. Some private insurers calculate co-pays based on a dollar amount. For example, you pay $5 for generics and $10 for preferred brands. If your doctor chooses a nonpreferred brand, then you pay $25. In some cases, you'll have no coverage for certain nonpreferred brands that are not on the formulary.

Drug Warnings

Co-pays can be your most expensive out-of-pocket cost. When considering plans, you must be sure you review your co-pays with initial coverage, as well as when you reach the donut hole. You'll find great variability in the costs for each drug from insurer to insurer.

Another common way that insurers set up their co-pays is based on a percentage. For example, you'll pay 10 percent of the costs for generic drugs and 25 percent of the costs for preferred brand-name drugs. Then, you could pay 50 percent of the costs for nonpreferred brand-name drugs. I take a closer look at these costs in Chapter 5.

Pharmacy Options

You can pick a pharmacy when searching for a plan, but I highly recommend that you don't choose that option. Private insurers sign contracts with pharmacies of choice. You'll get the best prices if you go to one of the pharmacies recommended by the insurer you pick.

Drug Tips

When you are searching for plans, check to see which pharmacies each plan accepts. If a plan does not include pharmacies near you on its approved list, consider a plan from another insurer that does work with a pharmacy you prefer.

Plan Types

Just to add to this confusion, you have two ways to get prescription coverage—a PDP and a MA-PD. Yikes, more initials to learn!

- PDP means a stand-alone Prescription Drug Plan. The average plan cost $37.29 per month nationwide in 2009, but there were options in some states for as low as $10.30 per month or more than $135 per month.

- MA-PD means a Medicare Advantage Prescription Drug Plan. Medicare Advantage Plans are an alternative to traditional Medicare. Most of these are health maintenance organizations (HMOs), which limit your choice of doctors. If you enroll in this type of plan, your prescription drug coverage would be included in that enrollment. Some plans charge no additional premium for drug coverage; others do charge an additional monthly premium. Medicare Advantage plans are much more complex and will not be discussed in this book. You can find out more about Medicare and Medicare Advantage Plans in *The Complete Idiot's Guide to Social Security and Medicare* (Alpha Books, 2006).

Premium Spreads

The cost per month, or premium, for Medicare Part D plans continues to increase each year. When the plans started in 2006, the average monthly premium was $25.93. The average plan in 2009 was $37.29—an increase of 43.8 percent. So even if you like the plan you are currently in, you should check out new options every year to be sure you are enrolled in the plan that works best for you.

Drug Tips

November 15 to December 31 is open season for these plans each year, and that's when you need to do your research and pick the plan that will result in the lowest annual costs based on the drugs you take. You should do this every year because plans not only change their premium costs, they also change which drugs will or will not be covered. Your drug needs may change year to year as well.

About 90 percent of the people who were enrolled in a Medicare PDP plan in 2008 faced higher premiums in 2009 unless they switched to a new plan, and about 25 percent of these folks faced an increase of $10 per month or more. That can make a big dent in a fixed-income budget.

The average retiree got a $63-per-month cost-of-living adjustment in her Social Security benefits in 2009. If her Medicare Part D premium goes up by $10, then almost 16 percent of that increase will go toward paying for drug coverage. Add to that the co-pays for prescription drugs and some seniors will end up with no increase to cover the inflation costs of food and other necessities.

Seniors saw significant increases in their monthly premiums between 2006 and 2009—in some cases as high as 329 percent. You should make a commitment to compare plans every year, because the one that will be the best price for you could change year to year.

Marketing played a big part in this premium price jump. Many insurers knew seniors tend to stick to the same plan year after year after they make their choice, so insurers priced the plans low in the first year to get the most enrollees. We'll talk more about marketing tactics in Chapter 3.

Plan Options Vary by State

The plan enrollment numbers might make you think there are only a few plans from which to choose, but that's not the case. In 2009, a total of 1,689 PDPs were offered nationwide, which was down from 1,824 PDPs in 2008. Some private insurers decided not to offer plans, some were asked to leave the market by the government because of management problems, and some individual insurers decided to offer fewer plans than in previous years. The number of PDPs offered in an area varies from a low of 45 PDPs in Alaska to 57 PDPs in the Pennsylvania/West Virginia region.

You might find the number of choices daunting to you. They are for most people. When you do your search using the Medicare tool online, you will likely find that you have at least 40 to 50 plans from which to choose. In Chapter 9, we'll show you how to use that tool to narrow your choices down and pick the best plan for you.

Gap Coverage

As I discussed earlier in the chapter, the donut hole or gap in coverage can result in thousands of dollars in out-of-pocket expenses. Some PDP plans do offer coverage in the gap, but the number of options dropped from 29 percent of the plans offering gap coverage in 2008 to only 25 percent offering coverage in 2009. Most of the plans offering gap coverage offer the coverage only for generic drugs. We'll talk more about the costs of drugs and the gap in Chapters 4 and 5. In Chapter 9, we'll show you how to use the Medicare tool to find the plans that cover the drugs you are taking.

Marketing of gap coverage has been unclear in some cases simply to attract customers, so in 2009 specific rules were mandated by the government to define marketing words. If you see the terms "some brand-name drugs" and "many general drugs," then the plan covers between 10 percent and 65 percent of brands and between 65 percent and 100 percent of generics in their formularies in the gap.

Even that attempt at defining marketing terms is weak, but it's better than in past years. Hopefully in the future, plans will have to identify more clearly what it is that they cover in the gap so people can make more informed choices about whether or not they want to pay for gap coverage.

The only way you can know for sure that you'll have coverage is to look at the formulary for each plan you are considering. You should call each plan you are considering and verify that your drugs are covered during the gap. The Medicare online tool can help you sort this out, but there can be mistakes in data entry when the list of drugs are input into the computer or insurers can change the list, so it's always best to double-check your individual drug list before you sign up.

Low-Income Subsidies

Some seniors qualify for low-income subsidies (LIS). Unfortunately, choices for low-income seniors are dwindling. In 2009, only 18 percent of the plans were available for LIS enrollees. That was down from 27 percent in 2008 and 24 percent in 2007. People who qualify for LIS pay $0 in premiums per month. I'll discuss qualifications for LIS in greater detail in Chapter 2.

Now let's take a look at who qualifies for Medicare Part D coverage in Chapter 2.

The Least You Need to Know

- When you're choosing a Medicare Part D drug plan, look at more than just the monthly premium. You must consider deductibles, co-pays, and drug costs when you're in the gap.

- Not every drug is covered by every insurer. You must check to be sure that the drugs you use are covered under the insurance plan you choose.

- Co-pays and prices for the drugs can vary greatly from insurer to insurer, so always look at the drug costs before you pick a plan.

- Some plans do cover your costs in the gap, or donut hole. If you expect your costs for your drugs to exceed $2,700, you may want to pick a plan with gap coverage.

Who's Covered

In This Chapter

- Enrollment qualifications
- Looking for creditable credentials
- Sign up cautions

Anyone who is enrolled or entitled to enroll in Medicare Part A or Part B is also eligible to enroll in Medicare Part D. But just because you're eligible doesn't necessarily mean that you should sign up.

In fact, of the 44 million people eligible for Part D, only about 17 million have signed up for Part D. Another 20 million or so get their drug coverage from another source and about 7 million don't have prescription drug coverage at all.

In this chapter, I'll review how you qualify for the prescription drug coverage. I'll also tell you whether or not you should apply if you do have other coverage available.

First ... the Qualifications

You are eligible if you meet one of the following criteria:

- You are 65 years old or older.
- You have been receiving disability payments from Social Security for at least 24 months.
- You have end-stage renal disease.

You're Eligible, but ...

You may fit in the category of being eligible, but don't apply too fast. Many of you who are eligible get your prescription drugs from other sources. You definitely don't want to rush to apply if you ...

- Are enrolled in a Medicare Advantage Plan.
- Get retirement benefits from a company or union.
- Get coverage from a State Pharmacy Assistance Drug Plan (SPAP).
- Get coverage under the Consolidated Omnibus Budget Reconciliation Act (COBRA).
- Get drug coverage from the Department of Veterans Affairs (VA).
- Get drug coverage from the Military Health Care System (TRICARE).

- Get coverage from Federal Employees Health Benefits (FEHB).
- Get coverage from Program of All-Inclusive Care for the Elderly (PACE).
- Get coverage from AIDS Drug Assistance Programs (ADAP).
- Get coverage for end-stage renal disease (ESRD).
- Qualify for Supplemental Security Income (SSI).

We'll take a closer look at each of these plans later in the chapter, but the general rule is that if you do get prescription drug coverage from somewhere else, check with your current provider to see if you need Medicare Part D or if your current plan is better than Medicare Part D before signing up for the new Medicare plan.

Is Your Plan Creditable?

You should get a letter from your current provider stating whether or not your plan is *creditable* by September of the current year before the open season for the next year starts in November. If you haven't received a letter, call your current plan to check about whether it is creditable or not. If your plan is creditable, that means that its coverage is at least as good as Medicare and may even be better.

def•i•ni•tion

Anyone over 65 who gets his prescription drug coverage from a source other than Medicare should become very familiar with the word **creditable**. Bet you haven't heard that one before. Basically, it means that your coverage is as good as or better than what is offered in Medicare Part D.

If you already have prescription drug coverage from a source other than Medicare, don't sign up for Medicare Part D before checking with your current provider of prescription drug coverage to see if you have creditable coverage. If you do sign up for Medicare Part D, you will likely lose your current prescription drug coverage automatically.

Look Before You Leap

Let's take a closer look at what you should do if you are eligible for Medicare Part D but receive prescription drug coverage from another source. I'll break down your actions by type of plan.

Medicare Advantage Plan

If you have enrolled in a Medicare Advantage Plan, then you likely will get coverage for your drugs from that plan. Check with your Medicare Advantage plan if you are not sure whether you have prescription drug coverage. As of January 2008, more than 8 million seniors got their prescription drug coverage through a Medicare Advantage Plan.

Employer or Union Plan

Most employers and unions who offer medical coverage to retirees offer prescription drug coverage as part of that coverage. In January 2008, more than 6 million retirees received coverage from their employer plans. Employers do get a subsidy from the government to entice them to include prescription drug coverage in retiree health plans.

The future doesn't look as rosy, though, for this coverage, which is usually better than what is offered under Medicare Part D. To save money, some companies are dropping retiree health coverage or at least coverage for prescription drugs.

Drug Warnings

Be very careful about signing up for Medicare Part D if you do have retiree coverage from your employer or union. Some employers say that retirees will lose both their employer-sponsored prescription drug coverage and their employer-sponsored medical coverage if they sign up for Medicare Part D. Do not sign up for Medicare Part D before talking with your employer or union about this.

SPAP

State Pharmacy Assistance Programs (SPAPs) still exist in only certain states. Some states are continuing to offer this plan, while others cancelled it when Medicare Part D started in 2006.

As of mid-2008, 42 states established or authorized some type of program to provide drug coverage or assistance. These subsidy programs, usually called SPAPs in most states, use state funds to pay for a portion of prescription drug costs based on enrollment criteria set by the state. Some programs offer discount or bulk purchasing programs but don't spend state funds on prescription drugs. Here's an overall breakdown of what's offered by the states:

- Thirty-eight states have enacted laws to create programs; others were created by executive branch action only, which means action by the governor but not the legislature.

- Thirty-two states have programs in operation as of June 2008.

- Twenty-two operational programs provide for a direct subsidy using state funds.

- Twenty-seven states created or authorized programs that offer a discount only (no subsidy) for eligible or enrolled residents. Some of these states also have a separate subsidy program.

- States that ceased operations of their SPAP programs and replaced them with Medicare Part D include Florida, Kansas, Michigan,

Minnesota, and North Carolina. Also, Medicare Part D replaced a discount plan in
Arkansas and South Carolina.

Drug Tips

If you're confused and want to know
how prescription drug coverage, as well
as other health insurance issues, are
being handled in your state, go to www.
statehealthfacts.org. This site is maintained
by the Kaiser Family Foundation and is an
excellent way to find out what is happen-
ing in each state regarding health care
and health insurance. You'll also find links
to key state health websites.

COBRA

If you have drug coverage through the Consolidated
Omnibus Budget Reconciliation Act (COBRA),
which is a health insurance plan that continues the
coverage you had through your employer for 18 to
36 months after you leave the job, check with your
insurer to see if your coverage is creditable. If your
coverage is creditable, you may want to keep the
COBRA coverage in place.

You must decide whether or not you want to keep
COBRA before enrolling in Medicare Part D.
Many COBRA plans will not let you drop your prescription drug coverage in that plan if you do want
to keep the coverage for your other medical needs.

If you do decide to keep your COBRA plan and it is not creditable, you will have to pay a penalty of 1 percent for each month you do not enroll in Medicare Part D, plus you will have to wait to enroll in Medicare Part D until the Annual Coordinated Election Period (November 15 to December 31 each year). I talk more about enrollment information in Chapter 6.

VA or TRICARE

If you receive your prescription drug coverage from the Department of Veterans Affairs (VA) or the Military Health Care System (TRICARE), your drug coverage is creditable and you don't need to sign up for Medicare Part D.

If for some reason you lose your VA or TRICARE benefits in the future, you will have 63 days after losing those benefits to sign up for Medicare Part D, as well as other parts of Medicare. If you miss the deadline for signing up, you will have to pay a 1 percent penalty, so don't delay. As soon as you know you are losing coverage, apply for Medicare Parts A, B, and D.

FEHB

If you receive your prescription drug coverage through the Federal Employees Health Benefits (FEHB), then your coverage is creditable and better than Medicare Part D. You probably do not want to enroll in a private Medicare Part D plan.

PACE

If you receive your prescription drug coverage through the Program of All-Inclusive Care for the Elderly (PACE), then do not sign up for Medicare Part D. You will lose your PACE coverage if you sign up for Part D.

PACE integrates Medicare and Medicaid financing, and offers both acute and long-term care services to those who qualify. PACE allows providers to deliver all of the services that participants need, rather than be limited to those reimbursable under the Medicare and Medicaid fee-for-service systems.

Participants in PACE must be at least 55 years old, live in the PACE service area, and be certified as eligible for nursing-home care by the appropriate state agency. The PACE program becomes the sole source of services for Medicare and Medicaid eligible enrollees. PACE providers assume full financial risk for participants' care without limits on amount, duration, or scope of services.

ADAP

Each state designs its own AIDS Drug Assistance Programs (ADAP), so you will need to contact your state to find out whether or not you should sign up for Medicare Part D. In some states the plans are creditable and even better than Part D. In other states the plans are not as good as Part D.

ESRD

If you receive your prescription drug coverage from Medicare because you are in end-stage renal disease (ESRD), contact your benefit specialist to determine whether or not you should sign up for Medicare Part D.

SSI

You also must be careful about how you sign up for Medicare Part D if you qualify for Supplemental Security Income (SSI) and get help with your Medicare Part B premiums. You must be sure you pick a plan that meets the requirements set by the Centers for Medicare and Medicaid Services. If you choose a plan with premiums that are too high, you will you have to pay out-of-pocket for the additional premium and possibly for co-pays. When selecting a plan, check with Medicare to be sure you are picking a plan that will give you fully paid coverage.

Your Next Steps

As you can tell, you must be careful about signing up for Medicare Part D if you have any type of prescription drug coverage already. Follow this general rule of thumb: if you have drug coverage, call your insurer and ask these two questions:

- Is my coverage creditable?
- Will my drug coverage continue when I turn 65 (if you haven't already turned 65)?

If the answer is "yes" to these questions, you likely don't need to apply for Medicare Part D. But you may want to search available plans and see if there is a plan that would provide better coverage than you now have.

If you do find you would be better off with Medicare Part D, then call your insurer and make sure you would not lose any other medical coverage you might have if you sign up for Medicare Part D. Sometimes insurers require you to have both basic medical and prescription drug coverage to be on their plans.

Now that you understand who qualifies and, even if qualified, who should and should not apply for Medicare Part D, the next chapter takes a look at insurers' marketing tactics and rules.

The Least You Need to Know

- If you're 65 or older, you're eligible for Medicare Part D, but be sure you want it. Your current prescription drug coverage may be better.

- If you do have coverage from another source for both medical care and prescription coverage, be sure you won't lose your medical coverage if you sign up for Part D.

- If you're covered for prescription drugs on another federal program, check with that program before signing up for Part D.

Marketing Tactics

In This Chapter

- Back to (marketing) basics
- Watching the marketers
- Permitted marketing approaches
- Agents and brokers

Federal expenditures for Medicare Part D prescription drug coverage totaled $44 billion in fiscal year 2008. That huge potential market provides an incredible opportunity for insurers to make money, so it's attracted a lot of competition for the bucks.

More than 1,500 different plans were available for 2009, with about 50 of those offered across most regions of the country. In this chapter, I'll review what the companies marketing Medicare Part D plans can and cannot do.

Marketing Basics

You need to know the basics of what plans are allowed to do so you can avoid getting caught up in a scam. Remember these five tips and you likely will avoid being ripped off:

- **Don't pay cash up front.** You never should agree to a cash-upfront payment. If a salesman asks you for a check, say no and walk away. The Medicare Part D program can be paid for in two ways. You can have the monthly premium taken out of your Social Security check (most people choose this method) or you can arrange for a bank draft. Under no circumstances should you be asked for a check on the day you sign up.

- **Door-to-door sales are not allowed.** Medicare Part D providers cannot sell their plans door-to-door. If someone comes to your door uninvited by you, refuse to let him or her in.

- **Telephone solicitations have limitations.** Most unsolicited calls about Part D plans are not allowed. I will discuss some exceptions later in the chapter, but generally if you haven't requested information or are not a current customer, the company cannot contact you. Just hang up the phone if someone calls you unsolicited.

Drug Warnings

Don't let anyone into your home or speak with anyone by telephone about Medicare Part D unless you have either invited the person to come or made a call asking for information. You must be the first person to contact the marketer. A marketer cannot contact you unsolicited.

- **Ask for credentials.** When you invite someone to your house to discuss a Medicare Part D plan, ask to see the person's credentials and company affiliation. Only talk with people who are representatives of Medicare plans approved by the Centers for Medicare and Medicaid Services (CMS). If you're not sure whether it is an approved plan before calling to set up an appointment with a particular insurer, you can call Medicare at 1-800-633-4227.

The most common type of fraud that has been reported has gotten the name "$299 Ring." In this scam, a caller identifies herself as representing a prescription drug plan, which ultimately turns out to be nonexistent. After talking the customer into signing up for this plan, the caller asks for an upfront payment of $299 from the customer's checking account.

Drug Tips

If you have a problem with a broker or agent, you can call CMS's special line for reporting fraud, waste, or abuse related to the Medicare Part D program at 1-877-772-3379.

Do not give the caller any information about your accounts. You may find that the dollar amount could be different from "$299," but it's still a scam. If you do get a call about this scam, call your local law enforcement officer or call the CMS at 1-877-772-3379.

Policing the Plans' Marketing Tactics

Luckily for all seniors, Congress passed the Medicare Improvements for Patients and Providers Act of 2008 (MIPPA), which included a provision that demanded CMS develop strict marketing guidelines for both Medicare Part D and Medicare Advantage plans.

Complaints about marketing tactics started flowing in to the CMS almost immediately after enrollments for the plan began in November 2005. Guidelines about marketing tactics had been around since enrollment in the Medicare Part D and Medicare Advantage plans started, but CMS had not been aggressive about dealing with these complaints—hence the new act (MIPPA) passed by Congress.

While the initial rules did stipulate that insurers are responsible for the conduct of their agents, even if the agent represents several different company plans, CMS did little to police the actions of insurers. In answer to Congress's demands through MIPPA, CMS promised better oversight for the 2008 open season from November 15 to December 31. Their new surveillance includes the following:

- Tripling the number of "secret shoppers" activities, in which a Medicare official poses as a prospective enrollee and monitors sales agents' presentations for inaccurate information and prohibited sales tactics.
- Reviewing local print and broadcast advertisements placed by the plans.
- Reviewing recordings of enrollment calls to ensure compliance with new regulations.
- Ensuring health and drug plans detect, report, and respond to agent/broker marketing misrepresentation and other issues.

Let's hope this stepped-up monitoring of the Medicare Part D marketers will end the abuse that has been seen in the past.

Exploring Marketing Tactics

Let's take a look at what's allowed and what's not allowed when plans initiate contact with you. This can be done at educational events sponsored by private insurers or at marketing tables set up in health-care settings. Other common practices include providing meals or gifts to get you to sign up for a sales appointment.

Contact with You

Unsolicited visits or calls from brokers or agents are the most common marketing complaints heard by Medicare advocates and by CMS. Under the new rules set for 2008, a company marketing Medicare Part D is not even allowed to call you to confirm if you've received information they've mailed to you. This prohibition includes plans and their representatives, which may be a third-party organization such as a drug store.

Third-party entities, such as a health website for seniors, selling leads that claim they are not unsolicited are not telling the truth. CMS has made it clear it will hold all plan providers responsible for the actions of their agents and brokers. Plans are still allowed to generate their own leads through mailings, plan websites, advertising, and public sales events, but leads coming from a third-party source are considered unsolicited leads.

The only type of unsolicited calls that a plan can make is to low-income subsidy-eligible members who are being reassigned to another plan to discuss plan options. CMS must approve call scripts for these calls.

Educational Events

Plans can hold both marketing events and educational events, but they must be clear on what type of event it is. If the event is advertised as an educational event, the plan or its brokers/agents cannot engage in marketing activities at the event.

If a third party organizes an educational event, such as at a senior center or a health center, then marketing activities are not allowed at the event. But if the event is not advertised as educational, then plan-specific information that complies with other marketing rules can be distributed.

Drug Warnings

Plans also cannot make contact with attendees of educational events in the parking lot or the lobby before or after an educational event. If you see marketing at an educational event, just avoid the marketers. Plans that don't play by the rules do not deserve your attention.

Marketing at Health-Care Centers

Plan representatives are permitted to make contact with you only in the common areas of health-care centers. These common areas can include hospital or nursing home cafeterias, community or recreational rooms, or conference rooms. Space outside the area where customers wait for services or to interact with the pharmacists can also be used for marketing by the plans as common area.

Plans cannot conduct sales activities in dialysis centers, exam rooms, hospital patient rooms, waiting rooms, or near pharmacy counters. If a patient is a long-term care resident, agents can make contact with the resident only if the resident has scheduled an appointment.

Drug Tips

Health-care providers may distribute marketing materials as long as they make available materials from all of the plans in which they participate. They can also display information describing the plans unless the plans fail to give the provider materials.

Providing Meals or Gifts

In previous years, you may have enjoyed a free meal or received a gift for listening to a marketing presentation. That is no longer allowed under the new marketing rules. Plans can serve light snacks at marketing events, but they cannot provide meals.

Plans can provide meals at educational events but cannot do any marketing at these events. If a plan representative wants to give a gift to people who attend a marketing event, the gift must be worth $15 or less—such as a magnetic calendar with the company name on it—and must not be convertible to cash. The plan also can't make it required that you enroll in the plan to get the gift.

Conduct at Sales Appointments

If you do set up an appointment with an agent, that agent must identify in advance the types of plans (or lines of business) they will discuss, such as prescription drug plans, *Medicare Advantage* plans, and *Medigap* plans. A salesperson can't make an appointment to discuss prescription drug plans and use it as a bait and switch to sell you a Medicare Advantage or Medigap plan. The salesperson must tell you all the plans she intends to discuss when she sets up the appointment.

def•i•ni•tion

Medicare Advantage plans provide more than just drug coverage. If you choose these plans, you will be giving up traditional Medicare and, in most cases, giving up the ability to choose any doctor. Most Medicare Advantage plans require you to only use doctors in their networks.

Medigap is an insurance plan that provides coverage for out-of-pocket expenses not covered by traditional Medicare.

If an agent made an appointment by telephone but did not record the call, then he must send you an appointment confirmation by mail, listing all the plans he intends to discuss and ask you to send back a signed form agreeing to the presentation before the meeting.

If you set up an appointment with an agent in response to an advertisement, then the agent can discuss only the type of plan that was advertised. If you do want to find out more about a plan that was not discussed prior to the appointment, then you will have to request the information and set up another appointment. The new appointment must be at least 48 hours after the first appointment.

For example, suppose you called a plan wanting information about prescription drug plans. When the agent comes to your home, he gives you information about a Medicare Advantage plan as an alternative. If the agent did not inform you at the time of setting the appointment that he planned to discuss Medicare Advantage plans, you would have to set up another appointment at least 48 hours later to discuss the Medicare Advantage plan in detail.

Agent/Broker Requirements

During the open season for Medicare Part D in 2006 and 2007, there were so many complaints about misconduct by agents and brokers that the Congress demanded CMS adopt stricter rules about agent training, testing, state licensing or certification, and compensation.

Training and Testing

Plans must train all contracted and staff agents or brokers annually about Medicare rules and regulations, as well as plan-specific coverage and procedures. Agents must also be tested and attain a score of 85 percent or better to pass and be allowed to sell the product. The tests are developed by each insurer for their agents.

CMS hopes that this required testing will reduce the number of misrepresentations in future sales. CMS assumes that in order to attain a passing grade of 85 percent or better, an agent would need to have a good working knowledge of the plans being sold.

State Appointment Laws

In order to sell a Medicare prescription drug plan in a particular state, an agent must comply with that state's laws concerning licensing and certification, as well as register an agent or broker (if required by that state). Plans or agents must pay any state appointment fees. Prior to 2008, agents and brokers had to comply only with the CMS to sell the prescription drug plans.

This new rule gives the states more control over the activities of agents and brokers in their particular states. States wanted this control because they believed that CMS did not have the manpower to adequately monitor agents' and brokers' actions. Hopefully this will give the states the power they need to crack down on misrepresentations to their own citizens.

Customer service representatives do not need to be state-licensed, as long as the scope of their activities is limited to answering questions with factual information, providing plan materials as requested by a potential customer, or completing enrollments for people who have already decided to enroll in a plan.

> **Drug Warnings**
>
> Starting on January 1, 2009, plans must report the termination of an agent or broker and the reasons for the termination to the state in which the agent or broker was appointed. This rule gives states a much better chance to police the actions of agents and brokers, and quickly recognizes the agents whose licenses should be pulled for inappropriate activities. Prior to this rule, unscrupulous agents could move easily from plan to plan using the same illegitimate tactics to make sales.

Compensation

For the first time, in 2008, CMS had to come up with rules to place limits on compensation so agents would not be enticed to steer Medicare Part D customers to plans that pay higher compensation but might not necessarily be the best option for the customer. New rules also attempt to stop "churning," which means to encourage customers to change plans each year just so the agent makes a higher commission.

At the time of this writing, rules were still being developed to answer these problems. The rules published so far stated that compensation for sales must be structured over a six-year period if the customer remains on the plan. The first-year commission may not exceed the renewal compensation by more than 200 percent of later years. Commissions were higher than that in the past and encouraged churning, which is getting seniors to change plans so the agents could earn higher commissions. Compensation may be changed if the beneficiary changes plans on his own in future years. But comments were still being taken about compensation and there could be changes in the final rule.

Drug Promises

In past years, plans claimed that many brand names or all generics were covered during the gap, but the customer would find out that wasn't true as she dealt with coverage issues through the year. To avoid any misunderstanding, CMS issued rules on when certain marketing terms could be used to promote gap coverage:

- **All**—A plan can use the word "all" only when 100 percent of drugs available on its formulary are covered through the gap. For example, if the plan says "All generics are covered," then every generic allowed under the plan's formulary must be included.

- **Many**—A plan that uses the word "many" must include 65 to 100 percent of the types of drugs covered through the gap, such as many generics.

- **Some**—A plan that uses the word "some" must include 10 to 65 percent of the types of drugs covered through the gap, such as some brands.

- **Few**—A plan that uses the word "few" must include more than zero and just under 10 percent of the types of drugs covered through the gap, such as few brands.

- **No gap coverage**—When you see the phrase "no gap coverage," it means that the plan offers zero percent coverage in the gap or covers less than or equal to 15 products in the gap.

Now that you understand what can and cannot be done to market Medicare Part D plans, the next chapter takes a closer look at how the plans structure the actual prescription drug coverage they offer and specify the drugs they will cover.

The Least You Need to Know

- A broker or agent cannot contact you unsolicited.

- You never need to pay anything upfront for Medicare Part D coverage, so if someone asks you for a check, refuse the plan and ask him to leave.

- Plans have strict limitations about how they can market plans. Get to know these limitations and avoid plans that are breaking the rules.

Controlling Your Drug Use

In This Chapter

- What's covered
- Formularies and tiers
- Limiting your drugs
- Appealing a drug decision
- Drugs that are not covered

While it's great to have help paying for your drugs, the biggest disadvantage of Medicare Part D is that you and your doctor no longer have total control over the best course of care. Often, an insurance company dictates the choice of drugs a person can be prescribed based on its formulary (the list of drugs that are covered).

You don't have a crystal ball, so you may not know when you choose a drug plan that you'll need to take a drug that isn't covered by the plan you chose. In this chapter, we'll review the rules regarding drugs that are covered and what to do if your doctor wants to prescribe a drug that isn't covered. Chapter 9 also presents further assistance with choosing the right plan for you.

Are Your Drugs Covered?

Everybody wants to know the answer to this question: "Will the drugs I'm currently taking be covered by the new Medicare Part D plan I select?" That is not an easy question to answer, and it depends upon the plan that you pick.

Before you start comparing plans, there are two key terms you need to understand about this new drug coverage—formulary and drug tiers.

Formulary

The formulary is a list of drugs the insurer will cover under the plan you have chosen. Each plan prepares its own formulary under the Medicare rules. You can find out a drug plan's formulary by going to the plan's website or by calling the plan and asking about the rules for each of the drugs you take.

Drug Tiers

Each drug on the formulary is assigned to a tier that will determine how much you will pay for the drug. Before signing up for a plan, make sure you know which tier each of the drugs you take is on. The amount you pay for the drugs out-of-pocket, both before the donut hole and in the donut hole, will be determined by its tier. Tier 1 drugs are the cheapest, and tier 3 or tier 4 drugs are the most expensive. If most of your drugs are tier 1 drugs, you have the best chance of avoiding the donut hole. I talk more about drug tiers in the following sections.

If a change in the drugs that you need occurs during the year, you may be able to get permission to use a drug not on the formulary and get coverage. Or you may have to take some drugs without coverage if your doctor thinks you need them. I talk more about appealing a drug decision later in the chapter.

Figuring Out Formularies

Medicare developed basic guidelines for the formularies. Each insurer must include drugs that are commonly used to treat common conditions. They must provide at least two drugs from each type or class of drugs. Medicare reviewed and approved the drugs listed in each plan's formulary.

You'll find both brand-name drugs (drugs sold by only one pharmaceutical company—the one that developed the drug), which are the most expensive types of drugs, and generic drugs (drugs sold by numerous pharmaceutical companies), which are cheaper than brand-name drugs.

For example, Toprol XL is the brand name for a drug commonly taken to lower blood pressure. The name for its generic equivalent is Metoprolol. Your drug costs will be cheaper if your doctor allows you to use the generic equivalent. Not all brand-name drugs have a generic equivalent.

Testing Out the Tiers

Once you find that your drugs are on the list, you then need to see what tiers they are in. The tiers determine how much you will have to pay for the drugs.

Private insurers use a two-tier, three-tier, or four-tier system. If the insurer you've chosen uses a two-tier system, you will likely find generic drugs in tier 1 and brand-name drugs in tier 2. If the insurer uses a three-tier system, you will find generic drugs in tier 1, preferred brand-name drugs in tier 2, and nonpreferred brand-name drugs in tier 3. Insurers that use a four-tier system include specialty drugs, such as expensive cancer treatment drugs, in tier 4. Tier 4 drugs can cost $600 or more per month.

In addition to the tiers, you will find that private insurers price the drugs in their tiers differently. Some insurers use a co-pay system based on dollar amount. For example, tier 1 drugs are $10, tier 2 drugs are $30, and tier 3 drugs are $60. If they do offer tier 4 drugs, the co-pays for those drugs can be $70 or higher.

The other pricing structure you may find is based on a percentage. For example, for tier 1 drugs you pay 10 percent of the cost, for tier 2 drugs you pay 20 percent of cost, for tier 3 drugs you pay 30 percent of cost, and for tier 4 drugs you pay 35 or 40 percent.

Limiting Your Drug Use

You may also find that the private insurer sets limits on the amount of a particular drug you can use. There are three ways an insurer can limit your use of a drug. It can …

- Require prior authorization.
- Limit the quantity you can take.
- Use a step approach.

Prior Authorization

For some drugs that you take, your physician may be required to get an authorization from the insurer for the drug before the plan will pay for it. Your physician will need to prove that you have a condition for which the drug is a standard medical treatment and that you have tried other drugs that are cheaper but didn't work.

Quantity Limits

For some drugs the common dosage is a certain number of milligrams (mg) per day, for example, one 10 mg pill per day. You may require a higher dosage than that, and so your doctor wants to prescribe 30 mg a day or three 10 mg pills per day. Your physician would have to explain why you need the higher dosage.

Step Approach

If a plan requires that you use the step approach or step therapy for a particular drug, you'll need to try using drugs to treat your condition based on the steps required by the plan for your health condition. In this case, the insurer is likely to require the simplest (probably the cheapest) drug first, then the next cheapest drug, and continuing up the steps until you find the drug that works best for you.

Checking on Coverage

Most people don't find out that they lack coverage for a particular drug until they go to the pharmacy to fill the prescription. Doctors don't keep all the formularies for all the drugs plans on file. It's a massive task to keep track of because most regions of the country have at least 50 plans from which to choose.

Drug Tips

If you want to avoid the problem of finding out at the pharmacy that you don't have coverage for a particular drug, then carry the formulary list with you when you go to the doctor so she can confirm that the prescription she plans to give you is covered. If not, she may be able to give you samples of the drug or prescribe something else.

If your pharmacist does tell you that you don't have coverage but the doctor still wants you to take the drug, your first step is to request a written coverage determination. You must have this written coverage determination before you can start an appeals process and ask for an exception.

Medicare has an official form that you can use called the coverage determination request form, which you can download at www.cms.hhs.gov/ MLNproducts/downloads/form_exceptions_final. pdf. You and your doctor should fill this form out together. It enables you to explain the medical necessity of the medication the doctor wants to prescribe.

The plan must respond to your written request for coverage determination within 72 hours, but your doctor can ask for an expedited response within 24 hours if medically necessary.

Getting an Exception

If you switch to a new plan that does not include one of your drugs or the drug formulary changed for the plan you are on, your plan must make sure you have the medically necessary drugs you need. The plan would need to work with you and your doctor to transition you from the drug you are using to one that is on the formulary.

Plans are likely to provide you with a 30-day supply of a drug you've been taking to give you and your physician time to either switch you to one of the drugs covered on the plan or give you time to request an exception to the formulary to cover the drug for you. Let's take a closer look at the process you need to follow to file an appeal to request coverage for a drug not on the formulary.

Requesting Permission to Use a Drug

In order to request a nonformulary drug, you must call or write the insurer (writing is better because you have proof of the contact) and also submit a written statement from your physician that says the prescription drug requested is medically necessary to treat your disease or medical condition. The plan would also need to know what other drugs have already been tried, how they worked, and how the nonformulary one is working. You can also use this process to request a lower co-pay, an exception to the number of pills you are allowed to take per month, or the dosage that is covered by the plan.

Plans must respond to your request for an exception within 72 hours. If the doctor believes there is a medical risk for you to wait 72 hours, the plan must respond in 24 hours or less.

Appealing a Decision

If you are denied the exception, then there is an appeals process, but you must appeal within 60 days of being denied. This first step is called a redetermination request.

The plan must respond to this redetermination request within seven days. If your case involves a medical risk, the decision must be made within 72 hours for an expedited appeal. If the redetermination request is denied, your plan must give you information about requesting a reconsideration by the Independent Review Entity (IRE).

Seeking a Reconsideration

You have 60 days after the appeals denial to request reconsideration from MAXIMUS Federal Services (www.medicareappeal.com), which is the third-party service that handles Medicare Part D appeals.

The IRE has seven days to respond to you. If you've filed for an expedited appeal, it must respond within 72 hours.

If the IRE also denies your request and the amount involved was more than $120 in 2009 (that amount changes annually), you are then entitled to ask for a hearing by an administrative law judge (ALJ).

Talking to a Judge

You must request a hearing before an ALJ within 60 days of getting a denial from the IRE for an amount in question that is more than $120 or the allowable amount in the year you are filing the appeal. The hearing normally will be scheduled for within 90 days, but it can take longer because there is no time limit set. Here's how it works:

- The Office of Medicare Hearings and Appeals will schedule your hearing and will tell you the time and place of the hearing.

- You participate in the hearing and give information about your case. Your health plan may also have someone at the hearing to give information. You can include anyone to speak for you or help you, including a family member, friend, or doctor. This person does not have to be a lawyer.

- The ALJ makes a decision based on your case file and the information given at the hearing.

- The ALJ sends the written decision to you, your health plan, and to MAXIMUS Federal Services.

- If the ALJ agrees with you, then MAXIMUS Federal Services will send a letter to your health plan telling it to pay or provide for your health care.

If you disagree with the judge's decision, you can then appeal to the Medicare Appeals Council.

Calling On the Council

You must contact the Medicare Appeals Council within 60 days after you get the judge's decision. The amount in question does not matter to ask for this appeal. The Medicare Appeals council is a board that is part of CMS and has no time limit. It can respond within whatever time period it needs. So, you have 60 days to appeal to the Council, but it has no time limit by which it must answer you.

Final Appeal—Judicial Review

If you disagree with the Council and the amount involved exceeded $1,180 in 2009 (that amount will change annually), then you can request a Judicial Review in federal court. You must file for that appeal within 60 days of getting a denial from the Medicare Appeals Council. The federal district court has no time limit within which it must respond.

If you total up all the steps in the appeals process, you will see it can take a year or more for the appeals process. By that time, you'll be eligible to change drug plans and hopefully find a plan that will cover the drug you need. Remember that you can change plans each year between November 15 and December 31. The new plan takes effect on January 1 of the next year.

If you want help with the appeals process, you should do the following:

- Call your local bar association or legal aid program. If you do not have much money, these offices may be able to help you with your appeal.

- Talk to a private lawyer who may charge you a fee.

- Call 1-800-MEDICARE to request the telephone number of your State Health Insurance Assistance Program.

Drugs Excluded by Law

You won't be able to get exceptions for all the types of drugs you may be taking. Some drugs are excluded from coverage by the law. These include the following:

- Nonprescription drugs or over-the-counter (OTC) drugs.
- Drugs used for the symptomatic relief of cough and colds.
- Prescription vitamins and mineral products, except for prenatal vitamins and fluoride preparations.
- Barbiturates (drugs used for sedation or to control seizures).
- Benzodiazepines (minor tranquilizers).
- Drugs used for anorexia (lack of appetite), weight loss, or weight gain.
- Drugs used to promote fertility. (Wonder how many seniors are thinking about that?)
- Drugs used to promote hair growth.
- Outpatient drugs for which the manufacturer requires tests or monitoring be purchased exclusively from them, such as certain anti-psychotic drugs.

If you are taking any of these drugs, you may be able to find a plan that offers enhanced alternative drug coverage. You will likely have to pay a higher premium to get this coverage.

Drug Tips

You can search for a plan that covers the drugs you take at the Medicare website. Medicare developed a powerful tool you can find at www.medicare.gov/MPDPF to help you locate a plan that covers the drugs you take. I take a closer look at how to use that tool in Chapter 9.

Finding a Plan That Covers Your Drugs

With all these stipulations, you're probably wondering how you can possibly find a plan that covers all your drugs. Luckily, that's not as difficult as you may think.

Medicare developed a powerful tool into which you can enter the drugs you take and get a list of all the companies that provide coverage for your medications, as well as the costs you can expect to incur out-of-pocket.

In Chapter 9, I take you step-by-step through the process of using this tool. If you're not computer savvy, ask someone to help you with a drug plan search or call your county's senior services office. Many senior service centers have counselors who can help you.

Where You Can Get Your Drugs

You will need to get your drugs from a pharmacy that is in the network of the plan that you pick. Medicare set the rules for how far that pharmacy can be from your house. If you live in an urban area, a network pharmacy must be within 2 miles of your home. If you live in a suburban area, a network pharmacy must be within 5 miles of your home. If you live in a rural area, a network pharmacy must be within 15 miles of your home.

The Medicare tool for selecting a plan allows you to specify your favorite pharmacy as part of your search for a plan. I recommend you don't specify a particular pharmacy, though, because you want to be sure you are getting the best plan at the best prices to meet your needs. Your favorite pharmacy may not contract with the plan that best meets your needs.

Now that you have a better understanding of the types of drugs covered by the plans and how to find out if a particular drug plan covers the drugs you are taking, let's take a look at the costs you can expect to incur for your drug coverage in the next chapter.

The Least You Need to Know

- Each Medicare Part D plan has its own list of drugs that it covers. If a drug you are taking is not on the formulary, the plan will not pay for the drug unless you get an exception.

- If your drug plan refuses to give you an exception, there are a number of steps you can take to appeal that decision.

- Some drugs are not covered by the Medicare Part D plan at all, but some drug plans provide enhanced coverage for these drugs if you want to pay for it.

Understanding Your Costs

In This Chapter

- Cost basics
- Comparing options
- Canada, anyone?
- Minimal drug use

Although most news articles about Medicare Part D plans quote the average premium price, that's not the most important number for you to consider. You must find the total annual cost of any plan you want to consider.

In this chapter, I show you what's included in the total annual costs of a plan and how to find that number. I'll also discuss what you should consider when determining your out-of-pocket prescription drug expenses.

The Bottom Line on Costs

When reading about the new drug plan, you've probably seen the monthly premium discussed most often. Do not choose a plan based solely on this number. Although the monthly premium could be low, the out-of-pocket costs when you pick up your drugs at the drug store each month could be a lot higher. That's because each drug plan negotiates its own drug prices and some are better than others at getting the best deal.

Drug Tips

When Congress passed the bill for Medicare Part D, Congress made it illegal for the government to negotiate drug prices, and all seniors are paying more for their drugs because of that decision. Hopefully Congress will change this rule.

Because drug costs can vary so much, the most important number you must consider when picking a plan is your total annual drug costs. Luckily, the Medicare tool for selecting a drug plan at www. medicare.gov/mpdpf figures out that number for you. Although there are sometimes problems with the pricing data in this tool, it's still your best option. I take you screen by screen to show you how to use the tool in Chapter 9.

Drug Tips

The best way to find a Medicare Part D plan is to use the online tool at www. medicare.gov/mpdpf. If you are not comfortable working with online tools, ask a family member or friend to help you use the tool. You also can get assistance with picking a plan by calling Medicare at 1-800-MEDICARE (1-800-633-2273).

Your total annual drug costs includes three elements—monthly premium, deductible, and co-pay. Let's take a closer look at each of these and the roles they plan in the annual costs of your drugs.

Monthly Premium

Your monthly premium is the amount you will pay monthly to buy the Medicare Part D benefit. It's similar to any insurance premium you pay. These premiums can change each year and sometimes go up dramatically.

The Kaiser family foundation found that 2009 premiums went up an average 18 percent over 2008 costs. Humana, the third-largest Part D plan, increased its premium by 51 percent in 2009 on average. Be sure to check your plan costs each year.

Premiums can be paid through monthly automatic withdrawal from your Social Security check (this is the most common way to pay for the drug cover-age), or you can arrange for the monthly premium to be taken out of your checking account.

Deductible

The deductible is the amount you have to spend out-of-pocket for drugs before you get any coverage. The most this could be in 2009 was $295. This amount has gone up every year since the drug plan started in 2006, when the deductible was $250.

Many plans offer a $0 deductible. Although this may sound good to you, avoiding the deductible is not always the best choice because the amount you pay for each drug during the year could be higher than a plan that requires you to pay the $295 deductible.

Co-Pay

A co-pay is the amount you will pay for each drug when you pick it up from the pharmacy. Co-pays vary greatly among the different plans out there. Remember, I discussed in Chapter 4 that co-pays are based on drug tiers and can be set as a dollar amount or a percentage amount.

Comparing Drug Plan Options and Costs

To help you learn how to sort out these complex elements, I developed a series of charts using the Medicare tool for the 2009 drug plan options. You can develop similar charts for the area in which you live. The tool enables you to compare up to three drug plans at a time. In my analysis, I found no advantage to using the plan with the highest premium.

I picked three cities for this comparison—Albuquerque, New Mexico (which has one of the cheapest monthly premiums at $10.30/month); Los Angeles, California (which has one of the highest monthly premiums at $129.30/month); and Brooklyn, New York (which has premiums in the middle, as low as $16.70/month and as high as $111.30/month). In each city I showed you the data for the plan with the highest premium, the lowest premium, and the best premium based on the drugs entered into the Medicare tool.

For this first chart, I used five common drugs used by seniors to get the total annual drug costs—Celebrex, Nexium, Plavix, Lipitor, and Advair. All of these are brand-name drugs and fall into tier 2, tier 3, or tier 4, depending on the plan.

For example, I found Celebrex as a tier 2 drug on only one plan. It was a tier 3 drug on five plans, and a tier 4 drug on three plans. On all nine plans (three from each city) I looked at, Celebrex was listed as a drug that might require prior authorization, step therapy, or quantity limits.

I found similar breakdowns for all five drugs I entered into the tool. In fact, Advair was not even on the formulary of three of the plans I included in this study, which means that if someone chose that plan and took Advair, he would have to pay for it totally out-of-pocket or ask for an exception. If a drug you are taking is not on the formulary of a plan you are considering, your best bet is to choose another plan. In all three cases in which Advair was not on the formulary, the plan was the lowest-cost option for the city.

In the following chart, you'll see a column for the city, the monthly premium, the deductible, the monthly co-pay before reaching the donut hole, the monthly co-pay in the donut hole, and the annual drug costs. The monthly co-pay column is what the senior would pay out-of-pocket each month to buy the drugs before reaching the donut hole and after the deductible is met (if there is a deductible). The donut hole column is the co-pay for the senior once she has reached the donut hole.

Total Annual Costs in Three Cities for Medicare Part D Using Five Common Drugs Taken by Seniors

City	Premium	Deductible	Monthly Co-Pay	Monthly Co-Pay in Donut Hole	Total Annual Drug Cost
Albuquerque—High Premium	$104	$0	$220	$629.02	$5,683
Albuquerque—Low Premium	$10.30	$175	$202.61	$657.44	$5,339
Albuquerque—Best Choice	$14.50	$295	$153.75	$631.02	$4,609
Brooklyn—High Premium	$111.30	$0	$220	$627.27	$5,770
Brooklyn—Low Premium	$16.70	$175	$204.61	$657.44	$5,416

continues

Total Annual Costs in Three Cities for Medicare Part D Using Five Common Drugs Taken by Seniors (continued)

City	Premium	Deductible	Monthly Co-Pay	Monthly Co-Pay in Donut Hole	Total Annual Drug Cost
Brooklyn—Best Choice	$20.80	$295	$170	$644.71	$4,694
Los Angeles—High Premium	$129.30	$0	$220.00	$642.21	$5,995
Los Angeles—Low Premium	$18.30	$175	$212.61	$657.44	$5,435
Los Angeles—Best Premium	$21.10	$0	$209	$634.75	$4,689

You can see that in all three cities the lowest premium did not translate to the lowest annual cost. That's because there is no coverage in the donut hole, so the amount that you pay for your drugs in the donut hole can have a significant impact on your total costs for the year. Your out-of-pocket costs for drugs both before the donut hole and while in the donut hole tend to be the lowest with the "Best" premium option.

Even if the premium or deductible is higher, which is the case with the "Best" options, ultimately the total you pay annually for the drugs you take tends to be the primary factor if you are taking mostly brand-name drugs. You can see, too, that it's a big mistake to choose the highest premium on the assumption that you'll get the most comprehensive coverage. The key factor in finding the best choice for the drugs used in this comparison was the total annual drug costs.

Drug Warnings

Don't be fooled by those attractive low-premium drug plans. Low premiums many times translate to higher costs for individual drugs, so the amount you'll spend out-of-pocket on drugs when you pick them up at the drug store will be higher and ultimately cost you more through the year.

In this scenario, with so many brand-name drugs on the list, the beneficiary would definitely reach the donut hole about halfway through the year. So it's critical to look at drugs costs not only when your co-pays are lower and the insurer is paying most of the costs, but also when you reach the donut hole and must pay for all drugs out-of-pocket. In Chapter 9, I'll take you through the steps you need to follow to find out the costs for your drugs.

Importing Drugs from Canada

We've heard many seniors say they find the Medicare Part D plan so confusing and expensive that they'll continue to get their drugs from Canada. I used the data collected in the previous drug plan comparison to develop the following chart that compares the cost of these five common drugs with Canadian prices. I did not include the high premium option in this chart, as those policies had the highest drug costs.

Drug Price Comparisons Between Medicare Part D Plans and Canada

Drug	Albuquerque —Best Premium	Albuquerque —Low Premium	Brooklyn —Best Premium	Brooklyn —Low Premium	Los Angeles —Best Premium	Los Angeles —Low Premium	Canada
Celebrex	$64	$50	$25	$48	$30.75	$47	$43
Nexium	$27	$22	$25	$20	$30.75	$20	$70
Plavix	$27	$22	$70	$20	$30.75	$20	$86
Lipitor	$64	$50	$25	$48	$30.75	$47	$39
Advair	$27	$68.61	$25	$68.61	$30.75	$68.61	$57

You can see that you can find a better option than Canada if you do your homework using the Medicare Part D tool. You will find the Canadian prices are cheaper when you get into the donut hole; however, the amount that you pay for your drugs from Canada will not be calculated in your total annual costs, so there would be no way to get out of the donut hole.

Drug costs fall dramatically when you do get out of the donut hole and reach the catastrophic coverage level. For the drugs shown in the table, the total cost per month for all the drugs after coming out of the donut hole was about $37. But if you started buying drugs from Canada when you reached the donut hole, you'd never be able to take advantage of the lower costs at the catastrophic level.

You can also determine whether or not you would get out of the donut hole by calculating out-of-pocket expenses in the donut hole. You need to total the costs you spend monthly and multiply that times the number of months you expect to be in the donut hole. If that number totals more than $3,453.75, then you will come out of the donut hole and will be able to take advantage of the lower cost at the catastrophic level.

Drug Tips

How do you know when you will end up in the donut hole? The Medicare.gov tool provides a chart that gives you that information. I'll show you how to find that chart and use it in Chapter 9.

Generics Will Save You Money

Using generics will save you a lot of money on all of the plans I used in this comparison, but the drugs I chose for our test are not available in generic versions. If you are taking only brand-name drugs, ask your doctor if there is a generic you can use instead.

You'll never end up in the donut hole if you take only generic drugs. In fact, trends show that more and more seniors are using only generic drugs, and that 64 percent of all drugs used by seniors are generics.

We checked the cost for one common generic drug used by seniors—hydrochlorothiazide (HCZT). One plan offered the drug with a co-pay of just $2.77 per month. Even the most expensive plan in our study required a co-pay of just $4.30 per month.

In some parts of the country, you will find plans that offer many generic drugs for $0, so be on the lookout for those as well. These plans are primarily regional (for example, offered in just one state or a tri-state area) rather than national plans.

What If You Don't Use Many Drugs?

Another myth we've heard among seniors is,
"I don't use many drugs, so it's not worth it to me
to pay a monthly premium for Medicare Part D."
I found three reasons that make this conclusion
wrong:

1. There is a penalty for late sign-up.

2. You can't sign up mid-year.

3. You'll still save money even if you don't spend
   much on your drugs without Plan D.

The Penalty for Late Sign-Up

Although you may not use many drugs today, you
don't know what your drug needs will be in the
future. If you don't enroll in Medicare Part D
within 63 days of the time you first become eligible,
you will pay a 1 percent penalty per month for each
month you delay for the rest of your life. For example, let's say you qualified for the Medicare Part D
in 2007 and decided not to enroll for the first two
years, or 24 months. That means your premium
will be 24 percent higher each year for the rest of
your life.

You Can't Sign Up Mid-Year

You can't enroll in Medicare Part D mid-way through the year, unless that is when you become eligible. Suppose you weren't taking any brand-name drugs during open season for 2009, so you didn't sign up for a Part D plan. Then in March you find out that you need to take two expensive brand-name drugs. You would not be able to sign up in the middle of the year, so you'd have to pay full cost for the drugs until the next year.

You'll Still Save Money

You'll likely find that even if your current drug costs are not high, you'll still find a drug plan that is worth it for you if you do your homework. Even if you take only generics, it's wise to have the protection, just in case you need more expensive drugs later.

The following chart shows you how this works. This chart uses the drug Nexium as its example, which can be bought from Canada for $70 per month or $840 per year.

Total Annual Costs in Three Cities for Medicare Part D for a Senior Using Only Nexium

City	Premium	Deductible	Monthly Co-Pay	Monthly Co-Pay in Donut Hole	Total Annual Drug Cost
Albuquerque—High Premium	$104	$0	$30	N/A	$1,608
Albuquerque—Low and Best Premium	$10.30	$175	$20	N/A	$550
Brooklyn—High Premium	$111.30	$0	$30	N/A	$1,695
Brooklyn—Low Premium	$19.60	$195	$39.40	N/A	$964
Brooklyn—Best Choice	$30.60	$0	$25	N/A	$705

City	Premium	Deductible	Monthly Co-Pay	Monthly Co-Pay in Donut Hole	Total Annual Drug Cost
Los Angeles—High Premium	$129.30	$0	$30	N/A	$1,912
Los Angeles—Low Premium	$18.30	$175	$22	N/A	$668
Los Angeles—Best Premium	$21.10	$0	$27	N/A	$615

You can see in this chart that you can find options that are better than buying from Canada. Even in comparison, you can also see that the lowest premium option would still cost you more based on your annual total drug plan costs in Brooklyn and Los Angeles. In Albuquerque, the best plan was also the lowest-priced plan.

The primary reason for the difference in costs was the premium. Although the co-pay did not vary that much for Nexium, the monthly premiums did. Another key deciding factor was whether or not there was a co-pay. When you take only one or two drugs, a $0 co-pay can make a big difference. You'll be safe if you choose the plan with the lowest total annual costs.

Now that you have a better understanding of the costs, let's review how you sign up for Medicare Part D and pay the premiums in the next chapter.

The Least You Need to Know

- Premiums are not the only things that impact your annual drug costs. You must also consider the deductible and co-pays.

- When you are choosing a plan, always choose the option that will give you the lowest total annual costs.

- Even if you only take one or two drugs, it's wise to sign up for a Medicare Part D plan.

Enrolling and Paying Your Premium

In This Chapter

- Enrollment methods
- Paying premiums
- Getting help with premiums

Once you've picked your plan, enrolling in Medicare Part D can be as easy as a phone call, but you do need to verify some information before finalizing your enrollment. You also need to make arrangements for paying the premium. If you can't afford it, you may be able to get "Extra Help." In this chapter, I tell you how to enroll, what to verify, and how to go about asking for financial help.

How to Enroll in Medicare Part D

The actual enrollment in the Medicare Part D plan is easy. Medicare Part D offers five different enrollment methods:

- Paper application—You can request an application from the company that interests you. In addition to the application, the company will send you complete information about its plan. Fill out the form and mail or fax it back to the company.

- Plan's website—You can apply for the plan of your choice on the plan's website. If you're computer savvy, you may prefer to read details about the plan online yourself before completing the online application.

- Medicare's website—You can use the tool on Medicare's website to pick a plan, and then apply for the plan you select right from Medicare's website. If you become an expert at using the tool that I show you in Chapter 9, you might prefer this option.

- Over the phone with Medicare—You can call 1-800-MEDICARE (1-800-633-2273) to talk to a customer service representative who can enroll you over the phone. You can also ask the Medicare representative to help you compare plans based on the drugs you take before deciding which plan you want to choose.

- Over the phone with the plan—You can call the private drug plan of your choice and enroll over the phone. A private drug plan cannot enroll you if it has called you. You must initiate the call if you want to enroll in a private drug plan. The only exception to this is if you are already in a private medical plan (Medicare Advantage) with the same company. In that case, the private plan can call you and enroll you in a prescription drug plan.

Although these are all valid options, your best bet is to research the plans online using the Medicare Part D tool. After you've picked your plan, call the private drug plan directly and review your medications with a customer service representative. Double-check with a representative to make sure all your drugs are covered, and then complete the application by telephone.

 Drug Tips

It's important to call and double-check your drug list before signing up. Drug formularies can be a moving target, and mistakes in entering drug lists can be made. By calling and double-checking the list of drugs you take, you can be sure to avoid choosing a plan that will not pay for one of the drugs you need.

How to Pay

You also must make a choice about how you want to pay for Medicare Part D. You can pay for Medicare Part D in three different ways:

- You can have the premium deducted automatically from your bank account.

- You can have the premium deducted from your Social Security benefits, similar to the way Medicare Part B is handled. This is the method most people choose.

- You can pay the drug plan directly by mailing the company a check or money order each month. This is probably the riskiest way to do it because if you forget to pay you could lose your coverage.

Drug Warnings

You must remember that you should never pay for a plan up front when you first sign up. If you are asked for cash up front and can't use one of the three payment options discussed, hang up and find another plan.

Getting Help If You Can't Afford to Pay

If you can't afford to pay for your drugs or your monthly premium, you may qualify for Medicare's assistance program, called "Extra Help." You can get help if you fit into one of these groups:

- Group 1: You have both Medicare and Medicaid and your monthly income is below $867 ($1,167 for couples). Your total assets must be below the Medicaid limits for your state.

- Group 2: You have both Medicare and Medicaid and your monthly income is above $867 ($1,167 for couples). Your total assets must be below the Medicaid limits for your state.

- Group 3: You have Medicare, but you do not have Medicaid. Your monthly income is below $1,170 ($1,575 for couples). Your assets are below $7,790 ($12,440 for couples).

- Group 4: You have Medicare, but you do not have Medicaid. Your monthly income is below $1,300 ($1,750 for couples). Your assets are below $11,990 ($23,970 for couples).

The income limits are adjusted each year based on the federal poverty level. The asset limits are adjusted yearly based on the consumer price index.

Your house and vehicles are not counted as part of your assets for this test. Burial plots or funds for burial up to $1,500 per individual also are not counted. Less than half of earned income is counted, so apply even if you think your income is too high.

Drug Tips

You may qualify with your income at a higher level if you take care of others. If you have someone in addition to your spouse living with you for whom you are responsible, you can add $3,600 annual income to the income limit for each additional person for whom you provide support.

If you qualify under Groups 1, 2, or 3, then you qualify for Full Extra Help. Your premium and deductible will be $0 as long as you choose a plan that offers basic coverage at or below the Extra Help Premium amount for your area. You can find that detail in the Medicare tool, but always double-check the information before signing up for a plan.

If you qualify for Group 4, then you are eligible for Partial Extra Help. The monthly premium you pay out-of-pocket will be based on a sliding scale. Your deductible will be $56 or the standard deductible your plan charges, whichever is cheaper.

The easiest way to apply for Extra Help is through Social Security by calling 1-800-772-1213 or filling out an application online at www.socialsecurity. gov/prescriptionhelp. But if you are denied help because of assets or income, don't give up. You may want to apply through your state's Health Insurance Assistance Program (SHIP). Some states have more lenient rules than others when calculating income and assets. Even after you get approved for Extra Help you still need to select a private plan and sign up for it.

Drug Tips

You can find contact information for your state's SHIP program on the Medicare website at www.medicare.gov/Contacts/static/allstatecontacts.asp.

If you qualify for Extra Help, here's what you'll get:

- Group 1: You do not have to pay a premium or deductible. Drugs cost $1.05 per generic drug and $3.10 per brand name. You have no co-pay after $5,726.25 in total annual drug costs.

- Groups 2 and 3: You do not have to pay a premium or deductible. Drugs cost $2.25 per generic drug and $5.60 per brand name. You have no co-pay after $5,726.25 in total annual drug costs.

- Group 4: Your premium is set according to a sliding-scale premium based on income and you pay a $56 deductible. Co-pays for this group are 15 percent, up to $5,726.25. If drug costs exceed $5,726.25, then co-pays are $2.25 per generic drug and $5.60 per brand name.

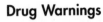

Drug Warnings

Be careful about which drug plan you choose if you qualify for Extra Help. If you choose a plan with a premium that is too high or that offers enhanced benefits, you will have to pay the additional premium or costs of benefits out-of-pocket.

In order to get full benefits from Extra Help, work with Medicare to find the private drug plan alternatives that meet the requirements of Extra Help for your area. The amount of help you get could differ depending on where you live. That extra phone call could save you a lot of money.

Applying for Extra Help

Filling out the application for Extra Help may look daunting, but take the time to complete it because it could save you a lot of money. Millions of people qualify for help but haven't filled out the application. Even if you're not sure, take the time to do it. The worst that can happen is that Social Security tells you no.

Before you even start filling out the application, pull together the following documents about your financial history:

- Most recent monthly bank statements
- Most recent payroll stubs (if working)
- Life insurance policy

- Investments
- Most recent tax return
- Pension letters detailing your benefits

You do not need to prove your income or your assets as part of the application process. You use the information you pull together to fill in the application—you won't have to send copies. But if you are married, you need to provide information about your spouse's income and assets even if you are the only one applying for Extra Help.

You can answer the questions on the application as though you are single if …

- You are married but living separately from your spouse.
- You have a domestic partner.
- You were married in a common law marriage.
- You are in a same-sex marriage that is recognized by your state.

You and your spouse should both apply on the same form if you are both eligible for Medicare and want Extra Help. If you don't plan to apply using the online system, then call Social Security to get a copy of the original form. If you download a form from the Internet, it could delay processing of your application.

Remember that you do not need to include the value of your primary residence or your car when listing your assets. If your assets are somewhat higher than allowed, you should still submit the application because you may have included something on the asset list that should not have been included.

You should always answer yes when asked if some of your savings will be used for burial expenses. If you answer no, then the asset limit for qualifying for Extra Help is lowered.

If you support relatives or have children (or grand-children) who live with you, be sure you include them in the count of people you support. You are allowed more income if you care for others.

If you are disabled, be sure to include information about your disability and any additional items you must pay for, such as a wheelchair or modifications to your car.

So, You Don't Qualify for Extra Help?

If you don't qualify for Extra Help but can't afford your medications, you still may be able to find resources for additional assistance.

Your first step should be to talk with your doctor to see if he or she can prescribe a low-cost generic drug rather than the brand name you are taking. Your doctor may also be able to give you free samples temporarily until a less expensive alternative can be found.

Working with your doctor, you also may be able to apply for an exception to formulary and get your Medicare Part D provider to pay for a drug not on the formulary. I talk about how to apply for exceptions in Chapter 4.

You also can ask your pharmacist for help. Some pharmacists will waive the drug co-pays on a case-by-case basis.

Some charities also help people with certain conditions. Charities that help with drug co-pays include the Caring Voice Coalition, the Chronic Disease Fund, the HealthWell Foundation, the Marrow Foundation Patient Assistance Program, the National Organization for Rare Disorders, Patient Advocate Foundation's Co-pay Relief, and Patient Services Incorporated. I give you a brief summary of the types of support they provide in the following sections.

Caring Voice Coalition

The Caring Voice Coalition helps with the cost of some of prescriptions if you have one of the following conditions: pulmonary arterial hypertension, idiopathic pulmonary fibrosis or Alpha-1 antitrypsin deficiency, chronic granulomatous, or Huntington's Disease. You can find out more about the assistance they offer at caringvoice.org or by calling 1-888-267-1440.

Chronic Disease Fund

The Chronic Disease Fund offers two types of assistance. The Patient Financial Assistance program provides co-pay assistance for certain drugs as long as your drug plan covers the drug but you cannot afford the co-pay. The fund also offers the Free Drug Program to people who meet income, asset, and medical condition guidelines.

The diseases for which the fund offers help include age-related macular degeneration, alcohol dependence, Ankylosing Spondylitis, asthma, breast cancer, colorectal cancer, growth hormone deficiency, multiple myeloma, multiple sclerosis, myelodysplastic syndrome, non-small-cell lung cancer, and psoriasis.

You can find out more information about the fund and the help it offers at www.cdfund.org or by calling 1-877-968-7233.

HealthWell Foundation

The HealthWell Foundation will help you pay your drug co-pays if you have insurance, or it will help you pay your monthly premiums if you are eligible for insurance but can't afford to pay for it. You must meet income criteria to qualify for help. The income criteria are based on income below 400 percent of the poverty level and are much higher than Medicare's Extra Help levels.

The foundation supports the following diseases: acute porphyries, age-related macular degeneration, anemia associated with chronic renal insufficiency or chronic renal failure, Ankylosing Spondylitis, asthma, breast cancer, carcinoid tumors, chemotherapy-induced anemia or nutropenia, colorectal carcinoma, cutaneous T-Cell lymphoma, head and neck cancer, Hodgkin's disease, idiopathic thrombocytopenic purpura, immunosuppressive treatment for solid organ transplant recipients, iron overload as a result of blood transfusions, non-Hodgkin's lymphoma, non-small-cell lung cancer, psoriasis, psoriatic arthritis, rheumatoid arthritis, secondary hyperparathyroidism, and Wilms' tumor.

You can find out more about the foundation at www.healthwellfoundation.org or by calling 1-800-675-8416.

Marrow Foundation Patient Assistance Program

The Marrow Foundation Patient Assistance Program provides assistance for the cost of pre-scription drugs that must be taken as part of recovery after a marrow transplant. To qualify you must have used the National Marrow Patient Assistance Program's donor registry to find your marrow transplant donor. Also, the donor must be someone who is not a family member.

You can find out more about this program at www.marrow.org or by calling 1-888-999-6743.

National Organization for Rare Disorders

The National Organization for Rare Disorders helps people pay for prescriptions they can't afford or helps pay for drugs not yet on the market. There are more than 1,000 diseases on the organization's database, so I can't list them all here.

To find out more about the diseases included in this program or to find out more about the organization, visit www.rarediseases.org or call 203-744-0100. You can leave a voicemail message at 1-800-999-6673.

Patient Advocate Foundation's Co-Pay Relief

The Patient Advocate Foundation's Co-Pay Relief pays your co-pay for prescriptions covered by your insurance as long as they are taken to treat a medical condition of interest to the foundation. Eligible conditions include breast, lung, prostate, kidney, colon, pancreatic, and head/neck cancers; malignant brain tumor; lymphoma; sarcoma; diabetes; multiple myeloma; myelodsyplastic syndrome (and other pre-leukemia diseases); osteoporosis; and selected autoimmune disorders and secondary issues as a result of chemotherapy treatment.

You can find out more information about this foundation at www.copays.org or you can call them at 1-866-512-3861.

You can see that there is a lot of help out there for people who can't afford their prescription medications, so don't just skip taking medications you need.

The Least You Need to Know

- You can enroll in your plan by telephone, by computer, by mail, or by fax.
- Be sure to double-check your drug list to be sure all drugs are covered before signing up.
- You may be eligible for extra help if you can't afford to pay your premiums or co-pay.
- If you can't afford your drugs, ask your doctor if he or she can prescribe a cheaper generic or help you file for an exception to get coverage for the drugs you need.
- Even if you're not eligible for Extra Help from Medicare or can't get an exception for the drugs you take, you may be able to get help from a private charity.

Chapter 7

Changing Your Plan

In This Chapter

- Changing drug plans
- Special reasons that allow you to change
- Discontinued drug plans

You can't easily jump in and out of prescription drug plans whenever you want. Most people can change plans only during the standard enrollment periods. However, there are some circumstances that warrant special consideration and allow you to change plans mid-year. In this chapter, I review how you go about changing your plans and when you can do it.

Standard Periods for Making a Change

In general, a person can change her prescription drug plan only during the two standard enrollment periods—Annual Coordinated Election Period or Open Enrollment Period.

Annual Coordinated Election Period

The *Annual Coordinated Election Period (ACEP)* for all prescription drug plans runs from November 15 to December 31 each year. New coverage starts on January 1 of the next year. Once you select a plan you must stay in that plan for a year—until the next ACEP.

def•i•ni•tion

Be sure to stay alert each year during the **Annual Coordinated Election Period (ACEP)**, which will be between November 15 and December 31 each year. That's when you can change your choice of private insurer for Medicare Part D.

Open Enrollment Period

If your prescription drug coverage is tied to a Medicare Advantage plan, you can also make changes during the annual *Open Enrollment Period*, which runs from January 1 to March 31 each year. During this period you can change your drug plan by changing your Medicare Advantage plan enrollment. You cannot add or drop drug coverage during this period, but if the new Medicare Advantage plan you choose includes drug coverage, then you would be switched to the new drug plan.

def•i•ni•tion

The **Open Enrollment Period** from January 1 to March 31 is for changing Medicare Advantage programs. You can switch your drug plan only if you switch your Medicare Advantage plan.

Switching for Special Reasons

Not all circumstances fit neatly into the standard enrollment periods, so Special Enrollment Periods (SEP) do exist. You can switch plans outside of the ACEP if …

- You move out of the area served by your current plan.
- You enter or leave an institution (such as a nursing home or assisted living facility).
- You lose creditable coverage through no fault of your own.
- You become eligible for creditable coverage.
- You choose to change employer or union coverage through your current or past employer.
- You are enrolled in a State Pharmaceutical Assistance Program (SPAP).
- You lose SPAP eligibility.
- You have Extra Help.
- You want to disenroll from a Medicare Advantage with drug coverage.

- You enroll or disenroll from the Program of All-Inclusive Care for the Elderly (PACE).
- You have had Medicare eligibility issues.
- You are eligible for a Special Needs Plan (SNP).
- You experience contract violations or enrollment errors.
- Your plan no longer offers Medicare drug coverage.
- You experience an "exceptional circumstance."

Later in the chapter, I'll take a closer look at what you need to do if you face any of these special circumstances. If you do face special circumstances, there will also be a Special Enrollment Period to give you time to work out these situations. Each type of situation has slightly different workout rules.

In most cases if you are seeking to start coverage after a special situation, you have two months from the start of one of these events to enroll in Medicare Part D. If you miss the deadline, you must pay a penalty of 1 percent of the premium per month for each month you miss the deadline for the rest of your life.

Move Out of Service Area

If you move out of the area served by your current plan or you move to a new area with more plans available, you will have an SEP to change Medicare

Part D plans. How long your SEP lasts depends upon how you give notice:

- If you notify your plan about the permanent move in advance, your SEP starts the month before your move and lasts up to two months after the move.

- If you notify your plan about the permanent move after your move, you have a SEP for two months beginning the month you provide notice of your move.

- If you did not notify your plan about a move and your plan learns about your move from the Centers for Medicare and Medicaid Services (CMS) or the post office, you will be disenrolled from your plan six months after your move. Your SEP begins on the sixth month and continues through the end of the eighth month after your move.

Your new coverage start day can begin the first day after the month you submit a completed application. You can also delay the start of coverage up to three months after your plan receives the complete application. That way, you can apply for coverage in the area to which you are moving before you move and have it in place when you get there.

Enter or Leave an Institution

If you enter an institution (including nursing homes, skilled nursing facilities, psychiatric hospitals, intermediate care facilities for the mentally retarded, rehabilitation hospitals, long-term care hospitals, and swing-bed hospitals), you can enroll or disenroll in Medicare Part D or you can change your Medicare Part D enrollment once a month.

After you move out of the institution, you have two months to enroll or disenroll from a Medicare Part D plan or to switch to another plan. Your new coverage will begin the first day after you submit an application.

Lose Creditable Coverage

If you lose creditable coverage through no fault of your own, or if your drug coverage on an employer or union plan is reduced so it is no longer as good as Medicare Part D, then you could qualify for a SEP. You don't qualify for an SEP if you lost drug coverage for nonpayment of premiums or if your financial circumstances change and you can no longer afford your payments.

In this situation your SEP for enrolling in a Medicare prescription drug plan begins the month you are told your coverage will end and lasts for two months after you lose your coverage or two months after you receive notice, whichever is later.

Your new coverage will begin the first day after you submit a completed application or up to two months after your SEP ends, if you request a delay in the start of your coverage.

Become Eligible for Creditable Coverage

If you've gotten lucky and can get prescription drug coverage from another source with creditable coverage, such as the VA, TRICARE, or a state pharmaceutical assistance program, you can disenroll from Medicare Part D as soon as you enroll in the alternative creditable coverage.

Change Employer or Union Coverage

You will be eligible for a SEP if you choose to enroll or disenroll from employer or union coverage through your current or past employer. During your SEP, you have three options involving employer or union coverage:

- Enroll in a new employer or union-sponsored Medicare drug plan
- Disenroll from a Medicare drug plan to take employer or union sponsored drug coverage
- Disenroll from an employer or union-sponsored coverage (including COBRA) to enroll in a Part D plan

With any of these choices, your SEP to enroll or disenroll in a Medicare Part D plan, or to switch plans, is the same time period that your employer or union normally allows you to make changes to your employee health-care coverage. If your employer or union coverage is ending, then the SEP ends two months after the month in which your employer or union coverage ends.

If you choose to enroll in Medicare Part D coverage during this SEP, your coverage can start up to three months after the month in which you submit a completed enrollment application. This allows you to apply for coverage as soon as you hear about a change and then pick a later date (up to three months later) for coverage to begin when you current plan ends. If your employer or union was late in sending in the notice of the change, your coverage may begin retroactively to when you submitted the application to the private Medicare Part D plan you choose, so keep a copy of what you submit and send it by certified mail so you have proof of the date you sent it in.

Enroll in an SPAP

If you are enrolled in a State Pharmacy Assistance Program (SPAP), you have a SEP to choose a new plan once per year at any time during the year. You cannot drop Part D coverage during this SEP. You also cannot take advantage of the SEP if your SPAP automatically enrolls you in a Medicare Part D plan. Your eligibility for coverage begins on the first day of the month after you submit a completed application.

Lose SPAP Eligibility

If you lose SPAP eligibility, you have a SEP to join another Medicare drug plan or another Medicare Advantage plan with drug coverage beginning the month you lose the SPAP eligibility and continuing

for two months after that. Your coverage begins the
first day of the month after you submit a completed
application.

Have Extra Help

If you have Extra Help (whether you applied for
it or got it because you have Medicaid, Medicare
Savings Program [MSP], or Supplemental Security
Income [SSI]), you get a SEP to join, disenroll
from, or switch Medicare drug plans beginning
the month you become eligible for Extra Help,
Medicaid, MSP, or SSI.

As long as you have Extra Help you can switch
plans once a month. But do not drop Medicare
Part D coverage if you have Medicaid. In most
cases you will lose your Medicaid benefits if you
disenroll from a Medicare Part D plan. If you are
on Medicaid, talk with your Medicaid counselor
before making any changes to your plans.

Drug Warnings

If you get Extra Help, Medicaid, MSP,
or SSI, call Medicare at 1-800-633-
4227 before making any changes to be
certain you don't do something wrong and
lose drug or medical coverage.

In most cases your coverage begins the first day
after the month you submit a completed application.
But if you have both Medicare and Medicaid or SSI

and are auto-enrolled in a plan by the CMS, then your enrollment may be retroactive to the first day of the month in which you qualified for Medicare drug coverage and Medicaid or SSI. You do have the option to choose your own Medicare drug plan instead of waiting for CMS to auto-enroll you, but if you want retroactive coverage to the first day of the month, you must request it.

If you lose Medicaid or MSP coverage, you have a SEP to switch plans that begins the month you lose that coverage and continues for two months after. If you do switch plans, the new plan starts the first day of the month after you submit an application.

Disenroll from Medicare Advantage Program

If you decide to disenroll from a Medicare Advantage program with drug coverage and go back to original Medicare, you get an SEP to join a stand-alone Medicare drug plan within one month of disenrolling. This SEP is available to you only if you are in the first 12 months of being on Medicare. Your coverage begins the first day of the month after you submit a completed application.

Enroll or Disenroll from PACE

If you enroll in a Program of All-Inclusive Care for the Elderly (PACE)—primarily nursing home care—you can disenroll from your Medicare Part D plan at any time. If you disenroll from PACE, you get an SEP to join a Medicare Part D program up to two months after the effective date of your disenrollment from the PACE program. Your coverage begins the first day of the month after you submit a completed application.

Medicare Eligibility Issues

If you have had Medicare eligibility issues, such as you received retroactive entitlement for Medicare and were not eligible to enroll in a drug program during your official initial election period, then your SEP to join a Medicare Part D plan for the first time begins the month that you receive notice of your Medicare entitlement and continues for two months after the month you get the notice. This most commonly happens when someone is out of the country at the time of initial eligibility or someone is in prison.

Your coverage starts the first day of the month after the plan receives a completed application.

Eligible for Special Needs

Some people are eligible for Medicare Special Needs Plans (SNPs). The plans are tailored for people with certain chronic diseases and conditions, such as diabetes or chronic heart failure; or who have specialized needs, such as people who have both Medicare and Medicaid; or people who live in certain institutions, such as nursing homes or inpatient psychiatric facilities. Medicare SNPs provide their members with all Medicare Part A (hospital insurance), Medicare Part B (medical insurance), and Medicare Part D services.

Drug Tips

Chronic conditions that are eligible for SNPs include diabetes, congestive heart failure, mental illness, and HIV/AIDS.

If you are eligible for an SNP, you can leave your Medicare Part D plan at any time to enroll in the SNP. The SEP ends when you join the plan.

If you lose eligibility to continue getting coverage through your SNP, you can join a stand-alone Medicare Part D plan beginning the month your special needs status changes. The SEP ends on your date of disenrollment from the SNP or three months after the effective date of your disenrollment if you are involuntarily disenrolled—whichever is earlier. The date your coverage starts depends upon your individual situation.

Contract Violations

If your plan violated your contract by failing to provide you with timely information about the benefits available or failing to provide benefits in accordance with set quality standards, or by giving you misleading information to get you to enroll in the plan, you get a SEP to switch to another Medicare drug plan once the regional CMS office determines that a violation has occurred. You can choose another Medicare drug plan during the last month of enrollment in your current plan. If you do not choose another plan immediately, your SEP is extended for 90 days from the time of your disenrollment from the plan that violated your contract.

Your new coverage begins in the new Medicare drug plan on the first day of the month following the month the new plan receives your completed application or up to three months after it receives your application. In some cases, CMS may process a retroactive disenrollment and/or a retroactive enrollment in another plan.

Drug Warnings

If you thought you were signing up for a Medicare Part D plan and got misled into joining a Medicare Advantage plan, call CMS (1-800-633-4227) immediately and complain. They can change your plan at any time of the year if they agree you've been misled.

Misleading Marketing

If you were misled into joining a Medicare Advantage plan when all you really wanted was a Medicare Part D plan, you will get a SEP to disenroll from your plan. You can then either return to original Medicare plus a stand-alone drug plan or join a different Medicare Advantage plan that includes a drug plan.

Your disenrollments and enrollments usually are effective the following month after the disenrollment request or completed application is received.

In some cases CMS may process a retroactive disenrollment and/or a retroactive enrollment into another plan.

Enrollment Errors

Ever since the Medicare Part D program started there have been complaints about misinformation and errors made by federal employees who answer the telephone at the CMS. If a federal employee made a mistake when completing your enrollment or disenrollment from a Medicare drug plan, you will get a SEP to change plans. Each time you talk with someone on the Medicare 800 number, write down the date, the name of the person you talked with, and the information you were told. That way you will have the proof you'll need for a SEP if they make an error and you want to request a SEP.

In this case, your SEP to enroll or disenroll in a Medicare Part D plan begins the month of CMS approval for the change and lasts for two additional months. Your coverage starts the first day of the month after you submit a completed application.

Plan Discontinues Drug Coverage

If your plan decides to discontinue offering Medicare drug coverage in the next year, you must get notification of its intent to stop coverage by September 30. Even if you do get that notice, your current plan must continue providing coverage through the current year of the plan.

If you get that notice, you will get a SEP to switch to another Medicare Part D plan beginning October 1 of that year until January 1 of the next year. You can choose to begin coverage under the new plan beginning November 1, December 1, January 1, or February 1.

If your plan discontinues coverage immediately and closes or changes its contract with CMS at any time of the year, you must be given at least a 60-day notice before that termination or modification of contract with CMS. In this circumstance, you will be eligible for a SEP to switch to another Medicare Drug Plan.

Your SEP starts two months before the proposed date of closing or plan modification and ends one month after the changes are set to occur. You can ask that your new plan coverage start the month after you get notice and up to two months after your old plan coverage ends.

CMS Terminates Your Part D Plan

In some cases CMS terminates its contract with a Medicare Part D provider. That termination can be in 30 days or it can be immediate.

If you get a 30-day notice, your SEP to switch to another Part D plan begins one month before termination occurs and lasts for two months afterward. You can choose to have your new plan coverage begin up to three months after the month your old coverage ended.

If CMS decides to terminate a plan's contract immediately, you will get notification of the termination and your SEP. This termination can happen mid-month. Your coverage for the new plan will begin the first day of the month after you submit a completed application.

Exceptional Circumstances

If your circumstance does not match any of the issues discussed here but you do have a problem with your Medicare Part D plan, call the CMS at 1-800-633-4227 and explain your problem. CMS has the right to grant a SEP based on "exceptional circumstances" and it never hurts to ask for one. If you are successful, then the length of the SEP and the start date for the new coverage will depend upon the circumstances.

The Least You Need to Know

- Most people who want to enroll in a stand-alone drug plan must do so between November 15 and December 31 for a plan that will start the next January 1.

- If you choose to join a Medicare Advantage plan with drug coverage, your open enrollment season is January 1 to March 31 each year.

- If you experience a change in circumstances, you may be eligible for a special enrollment period (SEP) outside of the standard enrollment times.

Chapter 8

Annual Reviews and Beyond

In This Chapter

- Yearly review of your coverage
- Rising costs of your drug plan
- Changing drug usage
- Plans for the future of Medicare Part D

You won't find anything easy about using Medicare Part D, but the good news is that it has helped a lot of seniors lower their drug costs. To keep your costs low, it's important to review available drug plans yearly.

In this chapter, I discuss why you must review your plans annually. I then explore how Medicare Part D is changing the ways senior use drugs, as well as examine changes to the law that are being considered by Congress.

Conducting a Yearly Review of Your Options

Once you've sorted through myriad options and completed your selection of a drug plan, I'm sure the last thing you want to think about is doing it all over again next year—but it's in your best interest to pay close attention to it each year.

Drug prices change yearly. In addition to the rising costs of prescription drugs, private insurers of the drug plans can change the provisions of their plans, raise their premiums, or raise their co-pays. They can also change the list of drugs that will be covered or in which tier your drug(s) may fall.

For example, suppose you're taking a brand-name drug that was on your plan's preferred list in 2008, but will be on tier 4 in 2009. Your costs for that drug can double or triple. (I talk more about what impacts the costs of drugs in Chapter 4.)

You should get a notice about changes in your drug plan between September and November each year. Most notices arrive in your mailbox in October, but if your provider will no longer be offering a drug plan in the next year, you should get a letter from them by September 30. I talk more about how to go about changing plans in Chapter 7.

If you get a notice that your plan costs are changing, you shouldn't just accept whatever premium increase you get. Be sure to check out all your options for your area each year to be certain you are getting the best drug coverage at the best price. In Chapter 9, I show you screen by screen how to use the tool at Medicare.gov to find the best plan for you based on the drugs you take.

If you're not comfortable using the Internet, ask a family member or friend to help you with the search. You can also get help at a senior center near your home. Call your county senior services coordinator to find local sources for help.

Drug Tips

If you don't now where to start to get help with your drug plan choices, call the Eldercare Locator hotline at 1-800-677-1116 or go to its website at www.eldercare.gov/Eldercare/Public/Home.asp. They will be able to point you toward local assistance centers.

Annual Premium Increases

The costs of Medicare Part D have risen each year since the program started in 2006. Following is a chart that compares costs on a year-by-year basis.

Comparison of Medicare Part D Costs from 2006 Through 2009

Benefits/Parameters	2006	2007	2008	2009
Weighted average premiums	$25.93	$27.39	$29.89	$37.29
Deductibles	$250	$265	$275	$295
Initial coverage limit before entering the gap	$2,250	$2,400	$2,510	$2,700
Maximum out-of-pocket costs before getting catastrophic coverage	$3,600	$3,850	$4,050	$4,350

You also may get a better deal by looking at some of the smaller drug plans. The most popular plans have increased their premiums rapidly now that they've captured a large percentage of the market. So those still trying to build market share may be more competitively priced in your area.

Forty-six percent of the 16.5 million people that enrolled in Medicare Part D chose one of just five plans. You will find at least 45 to 50 plans in most areas of the country. The five most popular plans increased their premiums dramatically during the period from 2006 to 2009.

Following is a chart that compares those five most popular plans.

Comparison of Premium Increases for Top Five Plans

Name of Plan	% of Enrollees	2006 Premium	2008 Premium	2009 Premium	% Change 2006–2009
AARP MedicareRx Preferred	16.6%	$26.31	$32.07	$37.03	41%
Humana PDP Standard	9.1%	$9.51	$25.52	$40.83	329%
Humana PDP Enhanced	8.7%	$14.73	$23.54	$38.21	159%
Community CCRx Basic	6.7%	$30.94	$24.93	$30.18	–3%
AARP MedicareRx Saver (not available in 2006)	5%	$14.43 (2007 premium)	$26.57	$28.69	99%

The plan with the most dramatic increase is Humana's PDP Standard, with an increase of 329 percent. The company low-balled its offering in the first year to capture as many subscribers as possible in the first year.

Based on market research done before offering the plan, insurers knew that many seniors tend to stick with the same plan if they are happy with it and don't tend to shop around. This has proven to be true, especially because Medicare Part D is confusing and so many people don't even want to think about doing another search for a plan.

Based on what I experienced helping people with sign-up for 2009 plans, Humana's dramatic price increase has sent a lot of people seeking help with finding a new private insurer. In addition to a dramatic increase in premiums, the two companies with the largest share of the marketplace—AARP and Humana—also cut some of the most popular brand-name drugs from their formularies.

As I was assisting people with their online searches during the annual enrollment period for 2009 drug coverage, I found that the AARP and Humana plans did not appear among the lowest costs options for people taking certain prescription drugs often used by seniors.

As I dug deeper into my research I found these drugs had been placed on higher, more expensive tiers, to discourage the choice of that plan. When a drug is placed on a higher tier, the co-pays are higher, and therefore, the total annual costs would be higher for a senior using those drugs. This strategy could cost AARP and Humana some customers, but they obviously don't want these customers who take certain expensive brand-name drugs, so they priced their services out of their reach.

Drug Warnings

Unfortunately, the millions of seniors who don't do a search annually will find that their annual drug costs rose dramatically in 2009 because most plans moved brand-name drugs to higher tiers or dropped coverage completely for some brand-name drugs.

When I did the drug cost comparisons in Chapter 5, the low-cost option did not include AARP or Humana in any state. That's because both insurers increased their monthly premiums and reduced the number of drugs they covered. In other cases, they moved many more expensive brand-name drugs to higher tiers with higher co-pays.

Drug Co-Pay Increases

In addition to premium increases from year to year, another key variable that can greatly increase your prescription drug costs is the co-pay for your drugs. You may find that a drug that was a preferred brand

and listed in tier 2 got moved to tier 3 or 4 with higher co-pays. When you check your prescription drug list against what is covered, you may even find that the prescription drug plan you were on this year will on no longer cover one or more of the drugs you are taking next year.

If that is the case, you have several choices:

- You can switch to a plan that covers all of your drugs—if you can find one.

- You can check with your doctor to find out if there is another prescription drug that you can take. There may be a generic available or there may be an alternative brand-name drug that your doctor can prescribe that's on the formulary of the plan you want to use.

- You can plan to seek an exception for the drug you are taking. I wouldn't recommend that you choose this option because you could be denied and then be stuck with a plan that won't cover a drug you need.

By checking your list of drugs before signing up for the next year you can avoid being stuck in a plan that will not pay for the drugs you need to take.

You may find that one or more of your drugs are so expensive that they fall in tier 4 for all plans, if they are covered at all. If that is the case, look for other types of help. You can find some special sources of help in Chapter 6.

Changing How Seniors Use Drugs

In order to save money, Medicare Part D's compensation structure encourages a shift to generic drugs. In 2008, 64 percent of all Medicare prescriptions were filled with generics, while 61 percent of prescriptions in the private sector were filled with generics. The number of seniors using generics is up by 8 percent since 2006 when Medicare Part D started.

Private insurers are driving this trend with the co-pay structure. Co-pays for generics are sometimes as little as $0 and can be as high as $7, while the co-pays for brand-name drugs usually start at $20 and can go much higher. Most seniors ask doctors for generic equivalents so they can reduce their drug costs and stay out of the donut hole, which is when they get no help with paying for their drugs.

Drug Warnings

Some doctors have been helping seniors stay out of the donut hole by giving them free samples of the more expensive drugs, but rumors are circulating in the senior community indicating that in 2009 the pharmaceutical companies may reduce the number of samples doctors have available. I have not confirmed these rumors, but they do persist.

The Office of the Inspector General for the Department of Health and Human Services found in their data collection of drug use for people on Medicare Part D that …

- Generic drugs were dispensed 88 percent of the time when generic substitutes were available. That gets very close to the Medicaid rate of 89 percent.

- Thirty-seven percent of prescriptions were written for drugs that have no generic substitutes compared to 41 percent for state Medicaid programs.

High rates of generic drug use help to minimize the costs for both seniors and the government, which pays the bulk of the actual costs of the drugs. The key losers are drug companies that develop new brand-name drugs.

Pharmaceutical companies fought hard against a plan to allow the government to negotiate discounts for brand-name drug use. As you may be aware, the United States pays the highest price for brand-name drugs worldwide because government-negotiated discounts in other countries reduce the cost of drugs by 40 percent to 50 percent in most cases. That's why people can buy drugs much more cheaply from Canada or England, where health care is nationalized and the governments have deals with the pharmaceutical companies.

In the United States, the pharmaceutical companies argued that they can't afford to continue the development of new drugs if the government can demand similar cut rates in the United States for drugs for seniors. So instead, the United States foots the bill for drug research for the world as other countries benefit.

Today each private Medicare Part D insurer must negotiate its own discounts with the pharmaceutical companies and drugstore chains—that's why you find such a great diversity in co-pays for each plan. This would not be the case if the U.S. government could negotiate a nationwide discount for all seniors, just like it does for all veterans through the Veterans Administration.

While preventing negotiated pricing by the government for Medicare Part D looked like a good strategy for the pharmaceutical companies, this strategy may be backfiring with the increased use of generic drugs.

Future Changes for Medicare Part D

With a new U.S. government administration under President Barack Obama and a greater majority of Democrats in Congress in 2009, expect changes to the Medicare Part D program to be enacted quickly. In fact, some may already have passed by the time this book makes it into print.

Congressional leaders were already discussing proposed changes for Medicare Part D to bring costs down and try to close the donut hole. One of the major changes being proposed will allow the U.S.

government to negotiate nationwide prices for drugs used by seniors in Medicare Part D. That could save a lot of money for both seniors and the government.

The other major change being considered involves overpayments to private insurers for Medicare Advantage programs. In 2009, as the law is currently structured, private insurers get an average of 13 percent higher reimbursements than are paid out to physicians under original Medicare. That will translate to about $10 billion dollars. By reducing those overpayments, Congress can find the funds it needs to close the donut hole.

Although insurers argue that these overpayments to Medicare Advantage enable them to offer better benefits to the seniors who choose them, actual studies have shown that seniors get a restructuring of benefits but that the actual outlay per senior is not that different. Most of the extra money collected by the private insurers goes instead to paying commissions for selling the insurance.

Medicare Advantage private insurers cannot cherry-pick their customers. All seniors must be eligible for all plans; they cannot be denied coverage. Private insurers have found a way around this, though. They discourage enrollments by people with chronic illnesses by not offering as high a reimbursement as they could get for their chronic illnesses under original Medicare. In some cases, some private insurers don't cover certain treatments at all.

For example, one person I helped in 2008 found out that he needed dialysis in March of 2009. He had switched to a Medicare Advantage plan in January of 2009. When he went for the dialysis he found out he had no coverage for it under the Medicare Advantage plan he chose. Luckily, in his case he was able to switch back to original Medicare because it was still open season. Had that happened in April, though, he may have been stuck without coverage for dialysis until the next open season unless Medicare granted him a special enrollment period.

If you are thinking about using a Medicare Advantage program instead of traditional Medicare because the costs appear cheaper, be careful. Before signing up for any plan, be certain that the treatments you need for any chronic condition will be covered.

Also, if you consider a Medicare Advantage program because the prescription drug costs are lower and they include some preventive care, check carefully through all benefits. For example, many Medicare Advantage programs are structured so that costs for going into a hospital are much higher under the Medicare Advantage program than they would be under original Medicare.

If you think it's difficult trying to sort out the benefits of Medicare Part D, it gets much harder to compare apples to apples when you look at the benefits of original Medicare vs. Medicare Advantage plans. Most Medicare Advantage plans are structured as HMOs and PPOs, which limit your choice of doctors. Others are private fee for service, but your doctor may not accept the payment terms and you may have to change doctors. So if you want to keep your doctors, always discuss the options you are considering with your doctor before switching away from original Medicare.

The Least You Need to Know

- Medicare Part D private insurers can increase your premium or change the list of drugs covered each year, so you should do an annual review of your drug plan options.
- The payment structure of Medicare Part D encourages the use of generic drugs.
- Congress could enact changes to Medicare in 2009 that will allow the government to negotiate drug prices for seniors and possibly close the donut hole.

Searching for Your Plan

In This Chapter

- Accessing the Medicare Part D search tool
- Entering the drugs you take
- Comparing drug plans
- Making your choice of plans

Now that we've discussed how Medicare Part D works and all its idiosyncrasies, it's time to search for your options, compare the options you want to consider, and finally pick the plan that is best for you. In this chapter, I take you screen by screen through the Internet Medicare tool so you can learn how to pick the plan with the best cost and options for you.

Accessing the Drug Finder Tool

You can access the search tool on Medicare's website at www.medicare.gov. When you get to the first screen (see Figure 1), you find a list of links in the middle of the page. You'll find links for Medicare Premiums and Coinsurance Rates, an online demonstration of the Prescription Drug Plan Finder, and the drug plan finder tool. The drug finder tool link for 2009 was called "Medicare Prescription Drug Plans—2009 Plan Data"; most likely the only change in the link for the tool in future years will be that 2009 will be changed to another date.

Figure 1

You can access the Medicare tool by clicking on "Medicare Prescription Drug Plans—2009 Plan Data."

You'll also see links for Medicare Health Plans. These are the Medicare Advantage plans. Many of the Medicare Advantage plans include prescriptions drugs, and if you want to use one of these alternatives to original Medicare, you would use this tool rather than the prescription drug tool.

Drug Tips

If you're finding it difficult to find plans that cover your prescription, you can use the Formulary Finder, but because the prescription drug plan tool permits you to enter your drugs and search for options, this is really an unnecessary step.

Starting the Tool

After you click on the link for the Medicare prescription tool, you go to a page that looks like Figure 2. From that page you can start the tool to find and compare plans that cover your drugs, you can enroll in a Medicare Prescription Drug Plan, or you can view your current plan.

You can also learn more about drug coverage options or about the plans in your area. We continue our journey by clicking on "Find & Compare Plans" to start the Medicare Prescription Drug Finder.

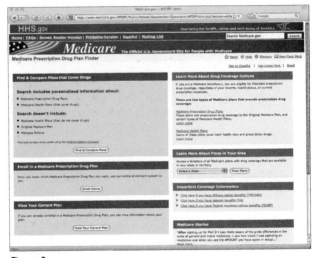

Figure 2

Click on "Find & Compare Plans" to begin your search.

Choosing the Tool

When you first start the tool, you're given the option to do a "Personalized Plan Search" or a "General Plan Search." You can see what that screen looks like in Figure 3.

I recommend that you choose the General Plan Search. I have heard from many people that when they try the Personalized Plan Search they find many glitches along the way. For example, they have trouble changing the list of drugs they take. Or, they seem to get locked into the plan they already have even though a better one may be cheaper for them.

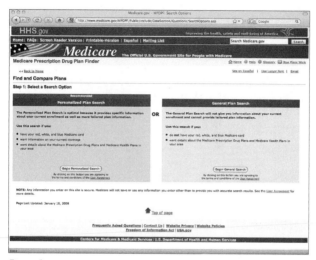

Figure 3

Choose to do a personalized search or a general search.

We continue our journey by clicking on "Begin General Search."

Targeting the Search

On the next screen (Figure 4), you target the search for your area by putting in your zip code. I selected a zip code in the south Florida area, where many seniors reside.

Next, you use the drop-down menu to select your age range. I chose 65–69. You may want to do the same even if you are older, so you're not caught up with questions about your current drug coverage. I tried using an older age and found glitches with the tool as I moved further into the process.

Figure 4

You need to fill in the blanks or answer the questions to target the tool to your area and your needs.

Next, you enter your health status using a drop-down menu as well. I picked Good for the purpose of demonstration.

Next, the tool asks if you currently have prescription drug coverage. Again, I recommend that you answer No even if you do have coverage. I have experienced problems when answering Yes. I also answer No to the question about other health insurance coverage, just to avoid problems with the tool.

Drug Warnings

In Chapter 2, I talk about people who should not consider Medicare Part D. If you fall into one of those categories, then you should not be searching for a Medicare Part D program. You could lose your current coverage.

The last question on this page is about whether or not you qualify for extra help. You should answer Yes if you do, so the tool will search for plans that qualify for extra help. For this demonstration I answered No.

When you finished answering the questions, click on Continue.

Review Your Answers

The next page (Figure 5) gives you a chance to review the answers you gave on the previous page. You'll also find the telephone numbers you can call if you want to get help that way rather than completing the search online.

You will also find a brief explanation about the rules for changing plans or possibly moving to a Medicare Advantage Plan. You'll also find links to pages that can help you learn more about Medicare Prescription Drug Plans and about how you can get extra help if you have limited resources.

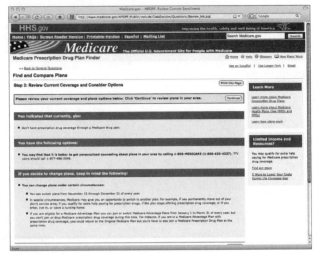

Figure 5

Review your selections. You can print out the page if you want to do so.

Once you have finished reviewing your answers, click Continue to go to the next screen.

Entering Your Drugs

When you get to the next page (Figure 6), you are given the option to enter your drugs or see available plans without entering your drugs. I highly recommend that you take the time to enter your drugs. The only way you can know if you're choosing a plan that covers all your drugs for the lowest possible annual costs is to take the time to enter your drugs.

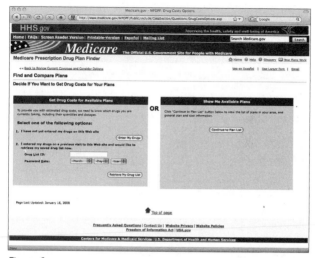

Figure 6

Choose the option to "Enter My Drugs."

If you've used the tool before, entered your drugs, and saved the entries, you will also be given an opportunity to retrieve the drug list already saved. To get to the next screen I click on "Enter My Drugs."

When you get to the drug entry page, you enter your drug name in the box next to "Enter Drug Name:" and click on "Search for Drug." A list of drugs similar to what you entered will appear.

As you can see in Figure 7, I entered "lipitor" in the box, clicked Continue, and then clicked on the appropriate drug in the search box that popped up to highlight it. Click on "Add Selected to Your

Drug List" to add the drug to the "My Drug List" box.

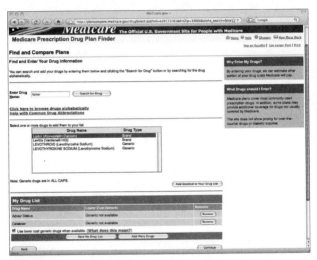

Figure 7

Enter your drugs one by one, select each drug by highlighting the appropriate one in the box that pops up, and then click "Add Selected to Your Drug List."

In the My Drug List box in Figure 7, you can see other drugs I already entered. As part of this demonstration I will enter the five drugs used in the drug cost comparisons done for Chapter 5. I am using a different zip code from Chapter 5 to give you an idea of drug prices in another area.

When you complete adding your drugs to the list, click on Continue at the bottom of the page.

Next, you get a screen that enables you to change the drug dosages and quantities of the drugs you take. You can see what this screen looks like in Figure 8. Some drug plans have formularies that limit the dosage you can take or the quantity of pills you can take, so be sure your drug list accurately matches your doctor's instructions.

In the Drug Name column you'll find drop-down menus that let you select the milligram dosages for your medications. In the Quantity/Days Supply column you can change the quantity to match the number of pills you actually take, and in the Actions column you can Add Doses or Remove a drug.

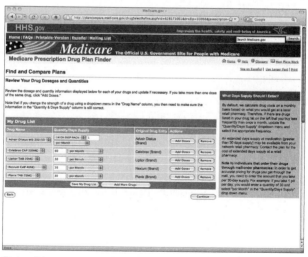

Figure 8

Adjust the drug list to match the dosage and quantities of pills you take for each medication on the list.

Once you've completed adjusting your drug list to match the way you actually take your drugs and the dosages you take, click Continue to go to the next screen. If you want, you are able to save your drug list (see Figure 9), but that's not required. If you don't want to save your list (I didn't), then just click Skip this Step and move to the next screen.

If you do want to save this list, which can take a long time to enter, you can start that save process by choosing a month, day, and year. Then click Continue.

Most people skip this step because they do not want to save a list of drugs. They just don't feel comfortable storing that information on the Internet.

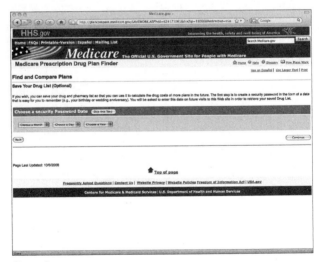

Figure 9

You can choose to save your drug list by choosing a security Password Date.

Next, you are given an option to select a preferred
pharmacy or pharmacies (Figure 10). I highly
recommend that you don't limit your options by
choosing a pharmacy. The key to the process is
finding the lowest cost for your drugs annually. If
the pharmacy you prefer is not on the preferred
list of the lowest price drug plan, you could miss a
good deal for you.

I check No, don't choose a pharmacy, and click
Continue.

Figure 10

*If you want, you can choose a pharmacy you prefer to use, but
I recommend not limiting your search.*

Comparing Plans

Whew! Finally after 10 screens you can start to compare drug plans. I didn't promise you this would be a simple journey, but it's definitely worth the time. You will save money finding the plan with the cheapest annual costs.

Comparing the plans on your personalized list you can see that this zip code has 54 Medicare Prescription plans available (see Figure 11). Imagine how much work you'd need to do to collect and read the information for that many plans!

You'll also see in the note on the screen under "Your Personalized Plan List" that 57 Medicare Health Plans (which means Medicare Advantage Plans) are available. If you want to go that route, you can click on that link. There are also eight plans that cover special needs in the zip code (these are primarily for people who qualify for extra help).

In Figure 11, you see only 3 of the 54 possible plans. There wasn't enough room to show you all the plans, but I will review the information shown in each column.

- Column 1 gives you the name and ID number of the plan.
- Column 2 gives you the estimated total annual cost for your drugs plus annual premiums. That's the most important number for you to consider when selecting your plan.

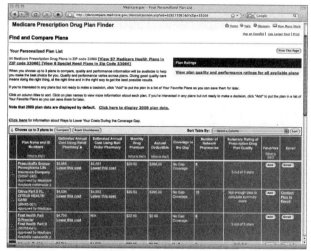

Figure 11

Review the plan options and pick three plans you want to compare.

- Column 3 gives you the estimated total annual cost if you use a mail order pharmacy. In some cases this could be a considerable savings.

- Column 4 is the monthly drug premium.

- Column 5 is the annual deductible.

- Column 6 tells you whether or not there is coverage in the gap. Most plans offer no coverage.

- Column 7 indicates the number of network pharmacies. If you find there is only one or two for the lowest price plan, check to be sure they are close enough to your house by clicking on the number in the column.

- Column 8 gives you an indication of the plan's quality rating based on CMS studies.
- Column 9 allows you to add the plan to your list of favorites.

Drug Tips

Since most areas of the country have at least 45 plans from which to choose, the full list can be very long. You may want to click on "add" in Column 9 to develop your own list of favorites that you can review later.

- Column 10 is a link to enable you to enroll online.

In Figure 11, you see that I put a checkmark next to the three cheapest plans in this search. You can only compare up to three plans at a time.

After you put checkmarks next to three plans that interest you, click on the Compare button at the top of the chart. If you picked three plans, but change your mind or want to compare additional plans, then click on "Reset Checkboxes."

You can compare as many plans as you would like, but remember that you can see the details for only three plans at a time. You may want to add the plans that interest you into your favorites (column 9) as you first scan through the list and then run the comparison of your favorites three at a time.

In Figure 12, you will see that instead of picking the three cheapest plans, I chose to compare the cheapest plan with no coverage in the gap, the cheapest plan with some generics covered in the gap, and finally the cheapest plan with gap coverage for many generics and few brands.

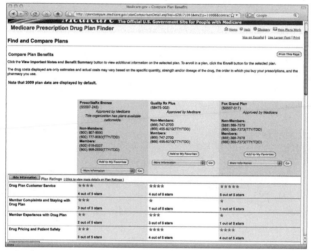

Figure 12

The top of the screen for comparing plan benefits.

In the boxes at the top of the comparison page you see the contact information for the plans. This includes two sets of numbers for each plan, one for nonmembers, which is the number you should call if you are not currently enrolled with that private insurer, and a second set of numbers for current members.

Next you see a box with ratings for customer service, member complaints, member experience with the plan, and drug pricing and patient safety. For example, you can see in this comparison the cheapest plan, PrescribaRx Bronze, gets four out of five stars for customer service and three out of five stars for member complaints. At the top of the ratings box there is a link you can click on to find more details about plan ratings and how they work.

Figure 13 takes you farther down the page. I clicked on Hide Information to hide the Plan Ratings section so I can show you some of the cost information for the three plans:

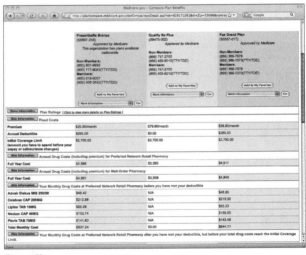

Figure 13

The middle of the screen for comparing plan benefits.

- PrescribaRx Bronze has the lowest premium of $20.90 per month, an annual deductible of $295 (which means you must pay that much for your drugs before coverage starts), and a total annual cost of $4,686. If you choose to use a mail-order pharmacy, the costs can be reduced by $35 to $4,651. This plan has no coverage in the gap.

- Quality Rx Plus has the highest premium of $79.90 per month, an annual deductible of $0 (which means your coverage starts immediately), and a total annual cost of $5,395. If you choose to use a mail-order pharmacy, the costs can be reduced by $36 to $5,359. This plan covers many generics and a few brands.

- Fox Grand Plan has a premium of $38.90 per month, an annual deductible of $285 (which means you must pay that much for your drugs before coverage starts), and a total annual cost of $4,911. If you choose to use a mail-order pharmacy, the costs can be reduced by $65 to $4,846. This plan covers some generics.

The next box on this screen shows the amount you'll pay for your drugs per month until you've satisfied your deductible. Because the brand names chosen for this example cost more than $295, all three plans would satisfy the deductible in the first month. In fact, coverage would start immediately for the highest premium plan, which has no deductible.

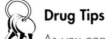

Drug Tips

As you compare prices for drugs, you'll see the lowest price plan, PrescribaRx Bronze, has negotiated slightly lower prices for each of the drugs than the Fox Grand Plan. Paying a higher premium does not necessarily mean you'll have lower drug costs.

In Figure 14, I move down the compare screen and look at the drug costs during the initial phase of coverage, the drug costs in the gap, and the drug costs after you come out of the gap.

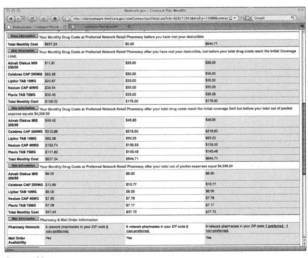

Figure 14

The middle of the screen for comparing plan benefits.

As you can see, the plan with the lowest annual costs, PrescribaRx Bronze, has the lowest monthly drug costs for these five drugs—$159.32. With the other two plans you will pay $175 after meeting the deductibles.

Why is that? As you compare the monthly costs of each of the drugs you'll see that Advair is just $11.61 on the cheapest plan, but $25 on the Quality Rx Plus, and $35 on the Fox Grand Plan. The Fox Grand Plan has the lowest monthly costs for Celebrex, but Quality Rx has the lowest costs for Lipitor and Nexium. The lowest cost for Plavix is on the Quality Rx Plus plan.

The next box shows the costs during the gap. You can see that the plan with the lowest costs, PrescribaRx Bronze, has the lowest monthly drug cost during the gap—$637.24. So, paying a higher premium for some coverage during the gap did not help in this case. Both of the other plans in this comparison have monthly drug costs in the gap of $644.71.

Drug Tips _____

The only way you'll know if it will help you to pay a higher premium for gap coverage is to put your drugs into the Medicare tool and do this type of search. The answer is different in every region of the country.

The final box on this page looks at monthly drug costs after you come out of the gap. The plan with the lowest annual costs and lowest premium also beats out the other two plans for lowest costs after the gap, but only by a few cents—$37.43 versus $37.72. In this comparison there is absolutely no reason to consider one of the two higher cost plans.

In Figure 15, I scroll lower down the page to see more detail to help explain these costs differences. You'll see in Figure 15 that I hid the detail you saw in Figure 14, which left room for the last two boxes on the screen.

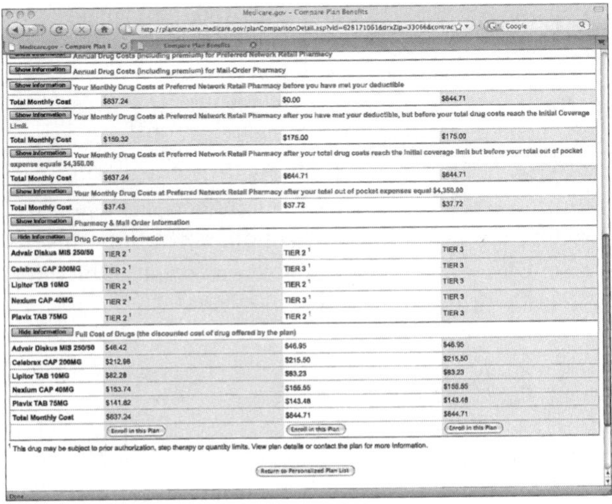

Figure 15

The bottom of the screen for comparing drug plans.

The Drug Coverage Information box details the tiers to help explain some of the differences in costs. The plan with the lowest annual costs places all the drugs on the list in tier 2, which are preferred brand drugs. That helps to keep the prices lower. Quality Rx Plus, in the middle, places some of the drugs in tier 2 and some in tier 3, nonpreferred brand-name drugs, which cost more. Fox Grand Plan, in the last column, puts all of these drugs in tier 3, which explains why most of the drugs cost more.

The box at the bottom of the screen details the discounted cost of the drugs offered by the plan. I don't find this box very useful because it matches information already given earlier in the table.

Making Your Selection

Now I assume you've compared all the plans you want to compare and are ready to make a selection of the plan that is right for you based on the drugs you are taking. For our example, I've chosen the plan with the lowest annual costs (PrescribaRx Bronze) even though I know I'll have to pay a deductible up front of $295. Its total annual costs are $4,686 at a preferred pharmacy and $4,651 using a mail-order pharmacy.

If you are on a fixed income and that deductible will be hard for you to meet, you may want to search for a plan with low annual costs that has $0 deductible. If you look back at Figure 11 you'll see that First Health Part D-Premier had a $0 deductible and a monthly premium of $22.90, just $2 more per month. The annual cost difference was just $14 per year—total annual cost $4,700 versus $4,686 for PrescribaRx Bronze.

Once you decide on your plan, hit the backspace arrow on your browser to go back to the page where you find and compare plans (refer to Figure 11) and click on the link to the plan that you've chosen. You'll then get a page that looks like Figure 16—Plan Drug Details.

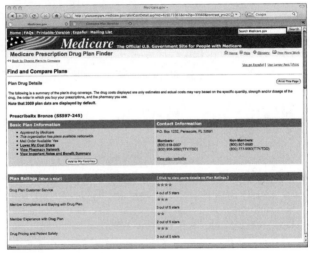

Figure 16

This image shows you the details of the selected plan in our example.

This screen looks similar to the information you got in the compare tool. In the Contact Information box you'll find a link to the company's website so that you can find even more detail about the company. The plan ratings box gives you exactly the same information as you saw on earlier screens about the plan.

When you scroll farther down the page (see Figure 17), you'll see the annual drug costs, which you've already seen on the comparison page. The most critical new information on this page is the Drug Coverage Information, which tells you if there are any restrictions on the drugs you're taking.

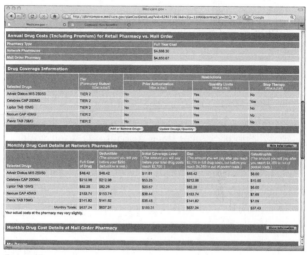

Figure 17

In this section of the screen, the most critical information is the Drug Coverage Information.

In my example, you can see there is no prior authorization required to take the drugs on the list, but all five drugs have quantity limits. If you see this on the drug plan you select, you should call the company and ask about the limits for each of your drugs before signing up.

When you call, you may find that there is no problem and the dosages you are taking fit into the company's criteria. But if you find out when you call that the company may question what your doctor prescribed, you will likely have to go through a procedure to apply for exception. If you find out that is the case, you may want to go back to the drawing board and do another search for a plan without those restrictions.

Be sure to check these restrictions before you close out of any search you do. If you find restrictions, print out the information for your first-choice plan and then look at your other choices to see if one would be a better match without restrictions. If you find all your choices have restrictions, then your only choice is to talk with the companies involved and find out more about the procedures for waiving those restrictions.

The bottom box in Figure 17 gives you a summary of all your monthly drug costs.

- Column 1 includes the drugs on your list.
- Column 2 shows is the full costs you'll pay for the drugs.
- Column 3 shows the amount you'll pay until you meet your deductible.
- Column 4 shows the amount you'll pay after you meet your deductible.
- Column 5 shows the amount you'll pay for your drugs when you are in the gap.

- Column 6 shows the amount you'll pay for
  your drugs when you come out of the gap
  and are getting catastrophic coverage.

When you scan farther down the screen, you'll see
Figure 18. The first box at the top right corner
shows the drugs and dosages you take. If you need
to change anything or want to add a drug, you can
do so there. But if you do need to make a change,
you probably want to redo your search to be sure
you've got the cheapest annual costs under the new
drug list.

You didn't select a pharmacy, so there are no pharmacies listed. You can check the list of pharmacies
if you go back to the main screen shown in Figure
11 and click on the number of pharmacies in column 7.

The box at the bottom of the screen shows your
costs through the year. In this scenario, you would
pay $407.58 for drugs and premium in the first
month. Then, you would pay $180.21 for months
two, three, and four. In month five, you would
enter the gap and pay $455.25. Part of your drugs
will be paid because you are not full in the gap that
month. In months six, seven, eight, and nine you
would pay $658.14, when fully in the gap. Finally,
in month 10 you would start to move out of the
gap and pay $533.61. As you move out of the gap,
part of your drugs will be paid. In months 11 and
12, you would have full catastrophic coverage and
pay just $58.33 for your drugs and your monthly
premium.

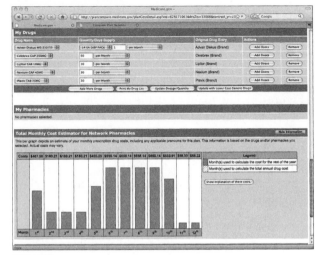

Figure 18

At the bottom of the Plan Drug Details screen, you'll find a chart that shows whether or not you will enter the gap.

Most people I work with who enter the gap do so in about the sixth or seventh month and never get out of the gap. That's true if you take two or three brand-name drugs. For a better understanding of the costs, review Chapter 5.

I highly recommended that you don't use the tool to sign up for a plan. While you can do so online, it's best to review your drugs by telephone with a customer service person from the plan you've chosen and make sure there were no errors in the data in the Medicare tool.

If you find the customer service person comes up with higher annual costs figures, you may need switch to one of your other choices. Don't let the person on the telephone try to sell you a higher-cost plan before you compare your total annual cost figures with your second and third choices that you found using the tool.

The screen-by-screen explanation for this book was developed in December 2008 with data to search for 2009 plans. If Congress does make changes to the plan, the tool could be slightly different for 2010 and beyond.

Hopefully, you found this screen-by-screen explanation helpful in picking the best plan. If after trying to use this tool you find it too difficult to do on your own, ask a family member or friend to see if he or she can help you. You can also contact a local senior center or your county senior services to see if there is a place you can go for assistance.

If there is no place near you where you can go for help, you can always call Medicare at 1-800-633-4227 and ask them to run a search for you.

The Least You Need to Know

- You can do a search online using the tool at Medicare.gov to find the lowest-cost plan for coverage of your prescription drugs.
- Take the time to enter all the drugs you take and adjust the dosages to match your doctor's orders before you search the Medicare tool for the cheapest plan for you.

- After finding the plan that appears the cheapest, dig down in the details to find your drug costs and whether there are any restrictions on the drugs you take.

Resources

Books

For more information on Social Security and Medicare, read *The Complete Idiot's Guide to Social Security and Medicare, Second Edition*, by Lita Epstein (Alpha Books, 2006).

For more information about prescription drugs, check out *Complete Guide to Prescription and Nonprescription Drugs 2009*, by H. Winter Griffith and Stephen Moore (Perigee Trade, 2008).

Websites

Centers for Medicare & Medicaid Services
www.cms.hhs.gov

This is a great website that includes research about all the programs offered under Medicare and Medicaid. You can find all the rules and regulations for each of the programs at this website.

Eldercare Locator
www.eldercare.gov/Eldercare.NET/Public/Home.aspx

Eldercare Locator is a public service of the U.S. Administration on Aging. The Eldercare Locator helps you find resources for older adults in any U.S. community. The website provides an instant connection to resources for seeking assistance with state and local area agencies on aging and community-based organizations that serve older adults and their caregivers.

Medicare
www.medicare.gov

You will find a treasure trove of information about all of the Medicare-sponsored programs on this website. You can also use this website to search available Medicare Part D plans and enroll in the plans.

Medicare Health and Prescription Drug Plan Tracker
www.kff.org/medicare/healthplantracker

The Henry J. Kaiser Family Foundation does an excellent job of tracking information about private Medicare plans nationwide. Go to this website to get details about what is being offered in your state and how it compares to other states.

Medicare Rights Center
www.medicarerights.org

This excellent organization advocates for people on Medicare. In addition to finding a wealth of information about Medicare basics and the center's advocacy activities, you can sign up for free newsletters from the Medicare Rights Center to stay on top of Medicare changes. Sign up for these newsletters online at www.medicarerights.org/about-mrc/newsletter-signup.php

State Health Facts.org
www.statehealthfacts.org

State Health Facts.org is another great website managed by the Henry J. Kaiser Family Foundation. You can use it to find details about health programs nationwide. This website not only gives you details about Medicare and Medicaid, but also about demographics and the economy, health status, health coverage and the uninsured, SCHIP, health costs and budgets, managed care and health insurance providers, minority health, women's health, and HIV/AIDS.

Important Phone Numbers

Drug Tips

If you experience a problem with a Medicare Part D salesperson or think you've seen evidence of fraud waste or abuse, call CMS's special line for reporting fraud, waste, or abuse related to the Medicare Part D program at 1-877-772-3379.

Eldercare Locator

If you need help finding senior services, you can speak to an Eldercare Locator information specialist by calling toll-free at 1-800-677-1116 weekdays, 9:00 A.M. to 8:00 P.M. (ET). Spanish-speaking information specialists are on duty.

Medicare Part D

If you want help choosing your plan by making a call rather than using Medicare's website, call 1-800-663-4227. Assistance is available 24 hours a day, seven days a week. English- and Spanish-speaking customer service representatives are available at this number to answer questions about Medicare plans and provide up-to-date information regarding the health plans available in your area.

Medicare Rights Center Consumer Hotline

If you want to talk with a Medicare counselor to get answers about health insurance choices, Medicare rights and protections, dealing with payment denials or appeals, complaints about care or treatment, or Medicare bills, then call the Medicare Rights Center's consumer hotline at 1-800-333-4114, between 9 A.M. and 6 P.M., Eastern Time, Monday through Friday.

Index